WORD PUZZLES

Willard R. Espy

D0840744

DEMBNER BOOKS
New York

Dembner Books
Published by Red Dembner Enterprises Corp.
1841 Broadway, New York, N.Y. 10023
Distributed by W. W. Norton & Company
500 Fifth Avenue, New York, N.Y. 10110

Text design by Antler & Baldwin, Inc.

Library of Congress Cataloging in Publication Data

Espy, Willard R.
    Word Puzzles.

    Includes index.
    1. Anagrams.   2. Word games.   I. Title
GV1507.A5E865   1983   793.73   83-14354
ISBN 0-934878-31-5 (pbk.)

Dedication

Some lost _ _ _ _ _ wandered through deep _ _ _ _ _,
So many wee Red Riding _ _ _ _ _.
The Ecklers saved the little stupes,
And taught them how to jump through _ _ _ _ _.

You will have no trouble filling in the missing words above once you have learned the simple rules for solving Doublets. But the Ecklers have no need to look up the rules—they will read the verse automatically, at first glance. The Ecklers let words know who is boss. That is why I dedicate this book to Faith and Ross Eckler, editors of *Word Ways*, with abiding admiration.

W.R.E.

The missing words: words, woods, Hoods, hoops.

Contents

Some suggestions (not too grim) about the most efficient way to solve these puzzle verses

The verses in the pages ahead were inspired, using that word loosely, by two familiar word games based on anagrams.

The first is the Doublet, popularized a century ago by Lewis Carroll.

The second is the Pyramid, which was doubtless born a split second after the written word itself.

—To create a Doublet, you replace one letter of a word at a time—each change making a new word—without rearranging the other letters. Your goal is a word that is either opposite to the first in meaning (as *black* is to *white*) or complementary to it (as *sty* is to *pig*). Harriet B. Naughton changed *sober* to *drunk* in thirteen moves, as follows:

> sober, saber, saver, paver, paves, pales, palls,
> pails, pains, paint, print, prink, drink, drunk

Darryl H. Francis shortened the number of moves required for that wordshift to nine by admitting two obscure words:

> sober, sorer, sores, cores, corns,
> coins, crins, crink, drink, drunk

(A *crin* is a heavy silk substance prepared from silkworm glue. To *crink* is "to make a thin, metallic, or cracking sound.")

—To make a Pyramid, you start with a one-letter word (generally A, I, or O, though you would be within your rights to begin, for example, "*M* is the first letter in *me*"). You then add a letter to make a two-letter word, and another to make a three-letter word, continuing in this fashion (juggling the letters as necessary, and making a new word each time), until you have gone as far as your ingenuity permits. Most people do not get beyond a word of nine or ten letters (and some of us wind up short of that), though legendary wordsmiths like Dmitri Borgmann have reached twelve, thirteen, or more. You can also reverse the procedure, taking a sesquipedalian word and reducing it step by step to a word of one letter. Here are a Pyramid and an inverted Pyramid:

A	FURTIVE
LA	VIRTUE
AIL	RIVET
LAIR	TIRE
TRAIL	TIE
TAILOR	IT
ORBITAL	I
LABORITE	
BALTIMORE	
IMPORTABLE	
PROBLEMATIC	

But you are not asked to turn one word into another in this book. I have done that for you, and fitted them into verses. All you have to do is figure out the words I used, which are represented by blanks. (The first puzzles are easy—but they get harder.)

These verse puzzles please me particularly because I have never come across anything quite like them. The nearest similarity is probably to the sort of anagram verses that Arthur Swan composed for many years for the Saturday Review of Literature, and that I contributed for thirteen months to Punch.* These earlier puzzles turn one word into another simply by rearranging its letters. Doublets and ESPYramids modify that procedure. Each move in Doublets replaces one letter of a word, the others staying in the same order as before. Each move in ESPYramids adds or subtracts one letter, and may or may not involve the rearrangement of the others.

The new modifications make it considerably easier to develop verses that have some excuse for being regardless of the puzzle element—which is why I present each entry first as a puzzle and then, on the overleaf page, in the clear. Inevitably, some of the constructs are more successful than others; but I hope that none will fail to provide you with a few minutes of amusement.

* The Punch puzzle verses appear, with some additions, in *Espygrams* (Clarkson N. Potter, 1982).

Your challenge as a solver is considerably less difficult than it may seem at first glance. There is only one really crotchety puzzle, in which identifying one word gives no clue at all to the likely meaning of the next. That is "What Does 'The' Mean, for Instance." I've put it at the end. Don't bother with it until you have solved all the others.

Go to work this way:

When doing a Doublet, first guess, from context and rhyme, what any one word is. Then work back and forth on the others. If the word you first fill in is at the start or end of the series, the one at the other end will (because it must be either complementary or opposite) probably reveal itself to you automatically. The rest, as a character says in one of my entries, is a piece of cake. (You will notice that some of my Doublets could be completed in fewer moves. I have taken a longer way around whenever I thought the added words helped the verse.)

The Doublets retain the name Lewis Carroll gave them, but I have changed Pyramids to ESPYramids to put my own brand on them.

You will find even more helpful hints in the ESPYramids than in the Doublets. The shortest word, consisting of but one letter, is self-evident; so is the two-letter word that follows and, in all likelihood, the one that follows that. So when you come to the fourth word, you are already three letters up. Difficulties may accumulate as the words get longer; but, as in the Doublets, you will have the title, the tenor of the verse, and frequently the rhymes to help you along. When the ESPYramid is descending rather than climbing, it will still be of help to identify the shortest words first, so as to have a start on the letters that make up the longer ones.

If you are temporarily stumped in solving an ESPYramid, you may wish to turn to "Clues," starting on page 187, where I have offered some help—but not too much. Then you can continue on your own.

It is quite possible, of course, that the solutions seem easy to me because I made the puzzles. If asked to solve the same sort of puzzle made by someone else, I might give up. But I don't think I would, and I don't think you will.

In fact I think you will have quite a pleasant time.

Doublets

Decide on the first missing word and turn it into the next by replacing one letter without rearranging the others. Continue in this fashion until you have determined the last missing word, which is the complement or the opposite of the first.

Below each verse/puzzle is a space, especially designed for that puzzle, in which to work out your solutions. (For this first puzzle you may not need it, but the work spaces may come in handy for the longer and more challenging Doublets ahead.)

Nursery Rhyme

Well, _ _ _ my kittens! _ _ _ _ my I's!
On my _ _ _ the old _ _ _ lies!

_ _ _
_ _ _
_ _ _
_ _ _

Nursery Rhyme

Well, dog my kittens! Dot my I's!
On my cot the old cat lies!

```
D O G
D O T
C O T
C A T
```

De Mortuis Nil Nisi Bonum

I noticed Joe give me the _ _ _;
He doesn't know my hair I _ _ _.
I'd die, I reckon, if he _ _ _;
Would he weep on my coffin _ _ _?

_ _ _
_ _ _
_ _ _
_ _ _
_ _ _

De Mortuis Nil Nisi Bonum

I noticed Joe give me the eye;
He doesn't know my hair I dye.
I'd die, I reckon, if he did;
Would he weep on my coffin lid?

E Y E
D Y E
D I E
D I D
L I D

But I'm Not Holding My Breath

If Porky _ _ _
Should don a _ _ _
And _ _ _ his snout
This _ _ _ about,
And _ _ _, "May I
Now leave my _ _ _?"
I think I'd die.

_ _ _
_ _ _
_ _ _
_ _ _
_ _ _
_ _ _

But I'm Not Holding My Breath

If Porky Pig
Should don a wig
And wag his snout
This way about,
And say, "May I
Now leave my sty?"
I think I'd die.

P I G
W I G
W A G
W A Y
S A Y
S T Y

Maybe My English Put Her Off

When it was _ _ _ down on the farm
We'd _ _ _ inside all snug and warm.
Once Jane and me _ _ _ on the _ _ _,
And she was _ _ _ but I was not.
I didn't mean to make her _ _ _,
And wouldn't of if it was _ _ _.

_ _ _
_ _ _
_ _ _
_ _ _
_ _ _
_ _ _
_ _ _

Maybe My English Put Her Off

When it was wet down on the farm
We'd set inside all snug and warm.
Once Jane and me sot on the cot,
And she was coy but I was not.
I didn't mean to make her cry,
And wouldn't of if it was dry.

WE T
S E T GET
S OT GUT
C OT GUY
C O Y
C R Y
D R Y

That Takes Some Youthful Vigor, Though

Men age, but women don't grow _ _ _.
It's _ _ _, but that's the way it is.
They do _ _ _ years, but still, I'm told,
Require no _ _ _ for monkey biz.
The _ _ _ of her is still for him;
Her _ _ _ is at the height he wishes;
She'll _ _ _ his line till sight grows dim.
What's _ _ _ with him? He does the dishes.

_ _ _
_ _ _
_ _ _
_ _ _
_ _ _
_ _ _
_ _ _
_ _ _

That Takes Some Youthful Vigor, Though

Men age, but women don't grow old.
It's odd, but that's the way it is.
They do add years, but still, I'm told,
Require no aid for monkey biz.
The aim of her is still for him;
Her hem is at the height he wishes;
She'll hew his line till sight grows dim.
What's new with him? He does the dishes.

O L D
O D D
A D D
A I D
A I M
H I M
H E M
H E W
N E W

He'd Kiss the Slipper That Kicks Him

"Oh, _ _ _ _ !" exclaimed the lovelorn lad;
"This _ _ _ _ is driving me quite mad!
But all the _ _ _ _ , should she enslave me,
I'd much prefer that no one _ _ _ _ me."

_ _ _ _
_ _ _ _
_ _ _ _
_ _ _ _

He'd Kiss the Slipper That Kicks Him

"Oh, damn!" exclaimed the lovelorn lad;
"This dame is driving me quite mad!
But all the same, should she enslave me,
I'd much prefer that no one save me."

DAMN
DAME
SAME
SAVE

Help Wanted: Alchemist, Good Wages

Of _ _ _ _ I have a _ _ _ _.
I'm told there is a _ _ _ _
That makes it turn to _ _ _ _.
(Well—that is what I'm told.)

_ _ _ _
_ _ _ _
_ _ _ _
_ _ _ _

Help Wanted: Alchemist, Good Wages

Of lead I have a load.
I'm told there is a goad
That makes it turn to gold.
(Well—that is what I'm told.)

L E A D   *LEND*
L O A D
G O A D
G O L D

Leave the Jabberwock Alone, Son

A Jabberwock is _ _ _ _ to slay—beware,
My beamish boy! A _ _ _ _ now, or a hare,
Makes snicker-snacking riskless. _ _ _ _ thou slain
A mouse, e'en? _ _ _ _ or _ _ _ _, the sane
Prefer the _ _ _ _ to the hard affair.

_ _ _ _
_ _ _ _
_ _ _ _
_ _ _ _
_ _ _ _

Leave the Jabberwock Alone, Son

A Jabberwock is hard to slay—beware,
My beamish boy! A hart now, or a hare,
Makes snicker-snacking riskless. Hast thou slain
A mouse, e'en? East or west, the sane
Prefer the easy to the hard affair.

H A R D
H A R T
H A S T
E A S T
E A S Y

But When He Feels Better,
He May Change His Mind

A man who's _ _ _ _ (though he in _ _ _ _ be dressed,
And though behind his _ _ _ _ such riches rest
As kings might envy) gladly would he _ _ _ _,
Nay, *give*, it all, if that would make him _ _ _ _.

_ _ _ _
_ _ _ _
_ _ _ _
_ _ _ _
_ _ _ _

But When He Feels Better,
He May Change His Mind

A man who's sick (though he in silk be dressed,
And though behind his sill such riches rest
As kings might envy) gladly would he sell,
Nay, *give*, it all, if that would make him well.

```
S I C K    SACK
S I L K
S I L L
S E L L
W E L L
```

I'm a Terror When I Get Mad

The blow I gave that Nazi's _ _ _ _
Won't _ _ _ _ for quite a spell.
" _ _ _ _ Hitler!" —that is what he said
(You'd _ _ _ _ me if I'd struck him dead!) —
And if he dares to leave his bed,
I'll tan his _ _ _ _ as well.

_ _ _ _
_ _ _ _
_ _ _ _
_ _ _ _
_ _ _ _

I'm a Terror When I Get Mad

The blow I gave that Nazi's head
Won't heal for quite a spell.
"Heil Hitler!"—that is what he said
(You'd hail me if I'd struck him dead!)—
And if he dares to leave his bed,
I'll tan his tail as well.

H E A D
H E A L
H E I L *TEAL*
H A I L *TELL*
T A I L *TALL*
        TAIL

"For Aye" Would Have Been Pretty Darned Long

"I'll _ _ _ _ you as long as we _ _ _ _," said she;
"I'll _ _ _ _ you in kisses for aye."
Oh, what could _ _ _ _ happened to her and to me
That she should so _ _ _ _ me today?

_ _ _ _
_ _ _ _
_ _ _ _
_ _ _ _
_ _ _ _

"For Aye" Would Have Been Pretty Darned Long

"I'll love you as long as we live," said she;
"I'll lave you in kisses for aye."
Oh, what could have happened to her and to me
That she should so hate me today?

```
L O V E
L I V E    HOVE
L A V E    HAVE
H A V E
H A T E
```

He Should Have Brought a Sail Along

On outboard motoring I'm _ _ _ _;
The _ _ _ _ slides through the water green,
      And O! I _ _ _ _ so masterful! . . .
But when the _ _ _ _ gives out because
I failed to check how _ _ _ _ it was,
      I find that rowing home is _ _ _ _.

_ _ _ _
_ _ _ _
_ _ _ _
_ _ _ _
_ _ _ _
_ _ _ _

He Should Have Brought a Sail Along

On outboard motoring I'm keen;
The keel slides through the water green,
    And O! I feel so masterful! . . .
But when the fuel gives out because
I failed to check how full it was,
    I find that rowing home is dull.

K E E N
K E E L
F E E L
F U E L
F U L L
D U L L

But We'd Ride Too If We Could

Brave fellows, come and lend a _ _ _ _;
We'll march as one to Kelly's _ _ _ _;
We lads are linked by such a _ _ _ _
As makes each one of t'others _ _ _ _;
Our drink we'll share, our _ _ _ _ divide,
And march by _ _ _ _ while rich men ride.

_ _ _ _
_ _ _ _
_ _ _ _
_ _ _ _
_ _ _ _
_ _ _ _

But We'd Ride Too If We Could

Brave fellows, come and lend a hand;
We'll march as one to Kelly's band;
We lads are linked by such a bond
As makes each one of t'others fond;
Our drink we'll share, our food divide,
And march by foot while rich men ride.

H A N D
B A N D
B O N D *BANE*
F O N D *BONE*
F O O D
F O O T

There May Be a Little Xenophobia Involved Here

In Oysterville, the water's _ _ _ _;
Of this we villagers are _ _ _ _.
But I'll acknowledge to you, _ _ _ _,
That just outside the town is _ _ _ _;
Depart no farther than a _ _ _ _,
And you will find the water's _ _ _ _.

_ _ _ _
_ _ _ _
_ _ _ _
_ _ _ _
_ _ _ _
_ _ _ _

There May Be a Little Xenophobia Involved Here

In Oysterville, the water's pure;
Of this we villagers are sure.
But I'll acknowledge to you, sire,
That just outside the town is mire;
Depart no farther than a mile,
And you will find the water's vile.

P U R E
S U R E
S I R E
M I R E
M I L E
V I L E

In Praise of Inebriety

However _ _ _ _ a man may seem,
A swig of _ _ _ _ will make him beam;
New kindness in his eyes you'll _ _ _ _;
He'll _ _ _ _ your heart with tender deed.
His evil's but an outer _ _ _ _;
A drink or two will make him _ _ _ _.

_ _ _ _
_ _ _ _
_ _ _ _
_ _ _ _
_ _ _ _
_ _ _ _

In Praise of Inebriety

However mean a man may seem,
A swig of mead will make him beam;
New kindness in his eyes you'll read;
He'll rend your heart with tender deed.
His evil's but an outer rind;
A drink or two will make him kind.

M E A N
M E A D — MEAD
R E A D — MEND
R E N D   MIND
R I N D   KIND
K I N D

Just Horsing Around

An old mare, feeling _ _ _ _ one night,
Implored her _ _ _ _ to snuggle tight.
This made him _ _ _ _; he left a note
And stowed away upon a _ _ _ _.
Next summer he came back all _ _ _ _,
And hugged the old mare in the _ _ _ _.

_ _ _ _
_ _ _ _
_ _ _ _
_ _ _ _
_ _ _ _
_ _ _ _

Just Horsing Around

An old mare, feeling cold one night,
Implored her colt to snuggle tight.
This made him bolt; he left a note
And stowed away upon a boat.
Next summer he came back all beat,
And hugged the old mare in the heat.

C O L D
C O L T   *HOLD*
B O L T   *HELD*
B O A T   *HEAD*
B E A T   *HEAT*
H E A T

Maybe It Will Grow Back

An old wolf sighed, "I've lost my _ _ _ _!"
I'm lying naked in my _ _ _ _!
I who laid tribute on the _ _ _ _,
Who led for years my thieving _ _ _ _,
Am _ _ _ _ and old, with none to care."

_ _ _ _
_ _ _ _
_ _ _ _
_ _ _ _
_ _ _ _
_ _ _ _

Maybe It Will Grow Back

An old wolf sighed, "I've lost my hair!"
I'm lying naked in my lair!
I who laid tribute on the land,
Who led for years my thieving band,
Am bald and old, with none to care."

HAIR
LAIR
LAID
LAND
BAND
BALD

But You Save on Gasoline

When Jack asked Jill to take a _ _ _ _,
She shook her head, and thus did _ _ _ _;
"Last night, behind a _ _ _ _ of hay,
You bade me do what no _ _ _ _ may;
This time at home I think I'll _ _ _ _.
To walk with you's to take a _ _ _ _."

_ _ _ _
_ _ _ _
_ _ _ _
_ _ _ _
_ _ _ _
_ _ _ _

But You Save on Gasoline

When Jack asked Jill to take a walk,
She shook her head, and thus did balk;
"Last night, behind a bale of hay,
You bade me do what no maid may;
This time at home I think I'll bide.
To walk with you's to take a ride."

```
W A L K     WALE
B A L K     BALE
B A L E     BILE
B A D E     BIDE
B I D E     RIDE
R I D E
```

Shower of Perseids

Hey man, that's real _ _ _ _ rock you hear, a-pounding in the sky!
A _ _ _ _ of stars above the _ _ _ _ are kicking up so high—
Are so besotted by that beat, that music of the spheres—
They sometimes slip and tumble down, and _ _ _ _ upon
       their rears.
The other stars won't _ _ _ _ a hand, but let them fall
       like _ _ _ _;
And when the stars fall down they die, and when they die
       they're _ _ _ _.

_ _ _ _
_ _ _ _
_ _ _ _
_ _ _ _
_ _ _ _
_ _ _ _
_ _ _ _

Shower of Perseids

Hey man, that's real live rock you hear, a-pounding in the sky!
A line of stars above the lane are kicking up so high—
Are so besotted by that beat, that music of the spheres—
They sometimes slip and tumble down, and land upon their rears.
The other stars won't lend a hand, but let them fall like lead;
And when the stars fall down they die, and when they die
   they're dead.

L I V E
L I N E
L A N E
L A N D
L E N D
L E A D
D E A D

My Burden Was Too Heavy to Bear

The living was _ _ _ _ in the _ _ _ _ that I _ _ _ _;
But my moll, though a doll, was too heavy to _ _ _ _;
The _ _ _ _ of my dagger protrudes from her breast—
As a _ _ _ _ from the hunter I flee from arrest;
It was too _ _ _ _ to lift her—to slay her seemed best.

_ _ _ _
_ _ _ _
_ _ _ _
_ _ _ _
_ _ _ _
_ _ _ _
_ _ _ _

My Burden Was Too Heavy to Bear

The living was soft in the loft that I left;
But my moll, though a doll, was too heavy to heft;
The haft of my dagger protrudes from her breast—
As a hart from the hunter I flee from arrest;
It was too hard to lift her—to slay her seemed best.

```
SOFT      SOOT
LOFT      SORT
LEFT      PORT
HEFT      PART
HAFT      HART
HART      HARD .
HARD
```

Well, Even Homer Nods

I know an expert on what's _ _ _ _;
He knows a mallard from a _ _ _ _;
Can _ _ _ _ who's short and who is _ _ _ _,
Which _ _ _ _ is true, and which is all
A pack of lies. Yet he will _ _ _ _
A true Van Gogh, and call it _ _ _ _.

_ _ _ _
_ _ _ _
_ _ _ _
_ _ _ _
_ _ _ _
_ _ _ _
_ _ _ _

Well, Even Homer Nods

I know an expert on what's real;
He knows a mallard from a teal;
Can tell who's short and who is tall,
Which tale is true, and which is all
A pack of lies. Yet he will take
A true Van Gogh, and call it fake.

```
R E A L     REEL
T E A L     REEL
T E L L     FEEL
T A L L     FEER
T A L E     FALL
T A K E       ·
F A K E
```

A Batty Tale of Malnutrition

Bats _ _ _ _ in a _ _ _ _ sadly cried,
"Though, _ _ _ _ it, we _ _ _ _ side to side,
Getting _ _ _ _ on the snout,
There are no gnats about
For the _ _ _ _ we need." So they _ _ _ _.

_ _ _ _
_ _ _ _
_ _ _ _
_ _ _ _
_ _ _ _
_ _ _ _
_ _ _ _

A Batty Tale of Malnutrition

Bats born in a barn sadly cried,
"Though, darn it, we dart side to side,
Getting dirt on the snout,
There are no gnats about
For the diet we need." So they died.

```
B O R N
B A R N
D A R N
D A R T
D I R T
D I E T
D I E D
```

TRUE

KISS

TELL

MISS
MESS
MIST
MAST
MALT
MALE
TALE
TALL
TELL

MALL
TALL
TE

He Had the Luck of the Oirish, Begorra

The kick of a mule landed _ _ _ _ in the _ _ _ _;
The scent wasn't _ _ _ _ where he found himself stuck.
He climbed from the _ _ _ _ with the help of a _ _ _ _ _
Who first scrubbed him clean and then gave him a _ _ _ _.

_ _ _ _
_ _ _ _
_ _ _ _
_ _ _ _
_ _ _ _
_ _ _ _
_ _ _ _

He Had the Luck of the Oirish, Begorra

The kick of a mule landed Mick in the muck;
The scent wasn't musk where he found himself stuck.
He climbed from the muss with the help of a Miss
Who first scrubbed him clean and then gave him a kiss.

```
K I C K
M I C K
M U C K
M U S K
M U S S
M I S S
K I S S
```

kick
Rick
Rice
Rise
Ruse
Muse
Mule

I Don't Even Catch the Strip Teases

I live in the _ _ _ _, and frequently _ _ _ _
The plays and ballets that surround me each night.
There isn't a _ _ _ _ of our cultural state
That my _ _ _ _ and myself could not claim as our _ _ _ _.
Yet our cultural _ _ _ _ is confined to TV;
Folks down on the _ _ _ _ have more culture than we.

_ _ _ _
_ _ _ _
_ _ _ _
_ _ _ _
_ _ _ _
_ _ _ _
_ _ _ _

I Don't Even Catch the Strip Teases

I live in the city, and frequently cite
The plays and ballets that surround me each night.
There isn't a mite of our cultural state
That my mate and myself could not claim as our fate.
Yet our cultural fare is confined to TV;
Folks down on the farm have more culture than we.

C I T Y
C I T E
M I T E
M A T E
F A T E
F A R E
F A R M

Too Good to Be True

He's _ _ _ _ of heart, the _ _ _ _ of guy
Who won't get _ _ _ _ or even try.
From every _ _ _ _ his goodness seeps;
If he must _ _ _ _ a pear, he weeps.
A _ _ _ _ 's more bellicose than he —
He's _ _ _ _ to like, at least for me.

_ _ _ _
_ _ _ _
_ _ _ _
_ _ _ _
_ _ _ _
_ _ _ _
_ _ _ _

Too Good to Be True

He's soft of heart, the sort of guy
Who won't get sore, or even try.
From every pore his goodness seeps;
If he must pare a pear, he weeps.
A hare's more bellicose than he—
He's hard to like, at least for me.

```
S O F T
S O R T
S O R E
P O R E
P A R E
H A R E
H A R D
```

SIFT. LOFT
LIFT LIFT
LIFE

SIFT

Better Hunt Up Those Prayer Beads

Your _ _ _ _ creaks, reluctant to respond;
It's _ _ _ _ where the muscles used to be.
Your _ _ _ _ to joys of which you've grown too fond
Has loosed—fine drinks, fine _ _ _ _, especially
Fine women. Time, old _ _ _ _, to look beyond.
You shuffle and you hack; your breath is _ _ _ _.
Flesh has betrayed you. Time to tend your _ _ _ _.

_ _ _ _
_ _ _ _
_ _ _ _
_ _ _ _
_ _ _ _
_ _ _ _
_ _ _ _
_ _ _ _

Better Hunt Up Those Prayer Beads

Your body creaks, reluctant to respond;
It's bony where the muscles used to be.
Your bond to joys of which you've grown too fond
Has loosed—fine drinks, fine food, especially
Fine women. Time, old fool, to look beyond.
You shuffle and you hack; your breath is foul.
Flesh has betrayed you. Time to tend your soul.

B O D Y
B O N Y
B O N D
F O N D
F O O D
F O O L
F O U L
S O U L

To the World's Worst Poet, in Fellowship

McGonagall, troubadour, _ _ _ _ in a _ _ _ _,
As _ _ _ _ got the _ _ _ _, but did not give a _ _ _ _.
Whatever his verse, it wound up in a _ _ _ _;
His fore lines were never in step with his _ _ _ _.
To Westminster Abbey he happily _ _ _ _,
Stretched out on the stones above Shelley, and _ _ _ _.

_ _ _ _
_ _ _ _
_ _ _ _
_ _ _ _
_ _ _ _
_ _ _ _
_ _ _ _
_ _ _ _

To the World's Worst Poet, in Fellowship

McGonagall, troubadour, born in a barn,
As bard got the bird, but did not give a darn.
Whatever his verse, it wound up in a bind;
His fore lines were never in step with his hind.
To Westminster Abbey he happily hied,
Stretched out on the stones above Shelley, and died.

```
B O R N
B A R N
B A R D
B I R D
B I N D
H I N D
H I E D
D I E D
```

Reflection for the S.P.C.A.

A _ _ _ _ man doesn't use a _ _ _ _
To drive his oxen down the _ _ _ _,
But shifts a portion of the _ _ _ _

To his own back. Yet, _ _ _ _, one fears
That man has _ _ _ _ between his ears—

What he finds _ _ _ _, the ox finds light,
And blows don't _ _ _ _ the beast a mite.

_ _ _ _
_ _ _ _
_ _ _ _
_ _ _ _
_ _ _ _
_ _ _ _
_ _ _ _
_ _ _ _

Reflection for the S.P.C.A.

A good man doesn't use a goad
To drive his oxen down the road,
But shifts a portion of the load

To his own back. Yet, Lord, one fears
That man has lard between his ears—

What he finds hard, the ox finds light,
And blows don't harm the beast a mite.

```
G O O D
G O A D
R O A D
L O A D
L O R D
L A R D
H A R D
H A R M
```

GOOD

EVIL

He Stayed a Bachelor

How _ _ _ _ was Simple Simon? True,
His cottage was a _ _ _ _
(The roof had leaks, the _ _ _ _ came through)
And yet there was a _ _ _ _ he knew,
Without a _ _ _ _, who used to woo
Young Simon with a _ _ _ _ *or two
(For instance, "thump" with "stump")
But could not make his ardor _ _ _ _.
In this, I think the fool was _ _ _ _.

*This is the old-fashioned spelling.

_ _ _ _
_ _ _ _
_ _ _ _
_ _ _ _
_ _ _ _
_ _ _ _
_ _ _ _
_ _ _ _

He Stayed a Bachelor

How dumb was Simple Simon? True,
His cottage was a dump
(The roof had leaks, the damp came through)
And yet there was a dame he knew,
Without a dime, who used to woo
Young Simon with a rime or two
(For instance, "thump" with "stump")
But could not make his ardor rise.
In this, I think the fool was wise.

D U M B
D U M P
D A M P
D A M E
D I M E
R I M E
R I S E
W I S E

But Maybe We're Better Off Without Him

He sure was one _ _ _ _ wire, that Joe—
A man in _ _ _ _ with life, by golly.
And always on the _ _ _ _, you know—
No quaking _ _ _ _ afraid of folly.
God broke the _ _ _ _ with Joe's creation—
Laid down his _ _ _ _, and said, "I win,"
And drank some _ _ _ _ in celebration.
But now Joe's _ _ _ _. God, that's a sin.

_ _ _ _
_ _ _ _
_ _ _ _
_ _ _ _
_ _ _ _
_ _ _ _
_ _ _ _
_ _ _ _

But Maybe We're Better Off Without Him

He sure was one live wire, that Joe—
A man in love with life, by golly.
And always on the move, you know—
No quaking mole afraid of folly.
God broke the mold with Joe's creation—
Laid down his meld, and said, "I win,"
And drank some mead in celebration.
But now Joe's dead. God, that's a sin.

L I V E
L O V E
M O V E
M O L E
M O L D
M E L D
M E A D
D E A D

Remember Avalon

How soft, how _ _ _ _ the wind did _ _ _ _
Through burning Camelot
Let memory now _ _ _ _;
How conqueror's _ _ _ _ and toady's _ _ _ _
Resounded, be forgot;
For Arthur's _ _ _ _ has done its _ _ _ _,
Has on the blazing _ _ _ _
His banner hammered _ _ _ _.
God—who could read such rot?

_ _ _ _
_ _ _ _
_ _ _ _
_ _ _ _
_ _ _ _
_ _ _ _
_ _ _ _
_ _ _ _
_ _ _ _

Remember Avalon

How soft, how slow the wind did blow
Through burning Camelot
Let memory now blot;
How conqueror's boot and toady's hoot
Resounded, be forgot;
For Arthur's host has done its most,
Has on the blazing mast
His banner hammered fast.
God—who could read such rot?


```
S L O W
B L O W    FLOW
B L O T    FLOG
B O O T    FLAG
H O O T    FLAT
H O S T    FLAT
M O S T    FIAT
M A S T
F A S T
```

. . . Then Pity, Then Embrace

Who'd not bewail the _ _ _ _ of such a _ _ _ _?
In honor she resisted every _ _ _ _;
_ _ _ _ days she lived by, when a woman's _ _ _ _
Was prudence. But her _ _ _ _ used cunning art—
Protested lust was love. His price she _ _ _ _;
The maid was _ _ _ _, and rose no more a maid.
The grasses wept their dew where she had _ _ _ _;
The virtue she had lost was vice's _ _ _ _.

_ _ _ _
_ _ _ _
_ _ _ _
_ _ _ _
_ _ _ _
_ _ _ _
_ _ _ _
_ _ _ _
_ _ _ _
_ _ _ _

... Then Pity, Then Embrace

Who'd not bewail the loss of such a lass?
In honor she resisted every pass;
Past days she lived by, when a woman's part
Was prudence. But her pard used cunning art—
Protested lust was love. His price she paid;
The maid was laid, and rose no more a maid.
The grasses wept their dew where she had lain;
The virtue she had lost was vice's gain.

```
L O S S        MOSS      LOST
L A S S        MASS      POST
P A S S        MAST      LAST
P A S T        MART      LAST
P A R T        PART      PART
P A R D        BARK      PARK
P A I D        LARK      LARK
L A I D        LARD      LARD
L A I N        LAID      LAID
G A I N        LAIN      LAIN
               GAIN      GAIN
```

No More Mr. Nice Guy

_ _ _ _ griped, "He bops me on the _ _ _ _,
And then he kicks me on the _ _ _ _;
He beats me till my senses _ _ _ _.
When once I _ _ _ _ a tale for food
He paid me with a lousy _ _ _ _."*
Then off he _ _ _ _. The Bible says
He should have _ _ _ _ his brother's ways.
Instead he crept on him _ _ _ _,
And wickedly killed _ _ _ _ dead.

*Even Shakespeare flubbed a rhyme once in a while.

_ _ _ _
_ _ _ _
_ _ _ _
_ _ _ _
_ _ _ _
_ _ _ _
_ _ _ _
_ _ _ _
_ _ _ _

No More Mr. Nice Guy

Cain griped, "He bops me on the chin,
And then he kicks me on the shin;
He beats me till my senses spin.
When once I spun a tale for food
He paid me with a lousy spud."
Then off he sped. The Bible says
He should have aped his brother's ways.
Instead he crept on him abed,
And wickedly killed Abel dead.

C A I N
C H I N
S H I N
S P U N
S P U D
S P E D
A P E D
A B E D
A B E L

Still, Brains Aren't Everything

What a silly lad is _ _ _ _!
Takes in love a stupid _ _ _ _:
Lots of _ _ _ _ and that is all!
Yet though he's not fair or _ _ _ _,
Little time elapses _ _ _ _
Jack has won the heart of _ _ _ _.

What a silly lass is _ _ _ _!
She can't make her mind up _ _ _ _
Someone neither fair nor _ _ _ _,
Who can _ _ _ _, and that is all,
Plops her heart down on a _ _ _ _,
Piercing her with love of _ _ _ _.

_ _ _ _
_ _ _ _
_ _ _ _
_ _ _ _
_ _ _ _
_ _ _ _

_ _ _ _
_ _ _ _
_ _ _ _
_ _ _ _
_ _ _ _
_ _ _ _

Still, Brains Aren't Everything

What a silly lad is Jack!
Takes in love a stupid tack:
Lots of talk and that is all!
Yet though he's not fair or tall,
Little time elapses till
Jack has won the heart of Jill.

What a silly lass is Jill!
She can't make her mind up till
Someone neither fair nor tall,
Who can talk, and that is all,
Plops her heart down on a tack,
Piercing her with love of Jack.


```
J A C K
T A C K    BACK
T A L K    BARK
T A L L    BALL
T I L L    BILL
J I L L    JILL

J I L L
T I L L
T A L L
T A L K
T A C K
J A C K
```

Envious Reflection Prompted by
the Dog Days of August

The carp are _ _ _ _, yet in their _ _ _ _
Beneath the hissing sun stay _ _ _ _.
The snakes, though broke, contented _ _ _ _,
And estivate* while humans boil.
_ _ _ _ isn't needed by the sweet
_ _ _ _ ripening to its _ _ _ _ in heat,
Or by the rice that, free of _ _ _ _,
Sucks up the sun. But O, how _ _ _ _
For my own _ _ _ _ to take advice
From fish or serpent, corn or _ _ _ _!
Instead we swelter. I would switch,
Though they are poor and I am _ _ _ _.

*Snakes don't estivate; they hibernate. But you would not deny
me my nip of poetic license, would you?

_ _ _ _
_ _ _ _
_ _ _ _
_ _ _ _
_ _ _ _
_ _ _ _
_ _ _ _
_ _ _ _
_ _ _ _
_ _ _ _
_ _ _ _
_ _ _ _

Envious Reflection Prompted by the Dog Days of August

The carp are poor, yet in their pool
Beneath the hissing sun stay cool.
The snakes, though broke, contented coil,
And estivate while humans boil.
Coin isn't needed by the sweet
Corn ripening to its core in heat,
Or by the rice that, free of care,
Sucks up the sun. But O, how rare
For my own race to take advice
From fish or serpent, corn or rice!
Instead we swelter. I would switch,
Though they are poor and I am rich.

```
P O O R        PooR
P O O L        DooR
C O O L          .
C O I L
C O I N
C O R N
C O R E
C A R E
R A R E
R A C E
R I C E
R I C H
```

He Was a Beast About Beauty

He _ _ _ _ _ every girl he dated;
He couldn't find a one that _ _ _ _ _.
He _ _ _ _ _ in dreams of perfect mates,
And _ _ _ _ _ the earth for candidates,
Yet _ _ _ _ _ none. (He was double-gaited.)

_ _ _ _ _
_ _ _ _ _
_ _ _ _ _
_ _ _ _ _
_ _ _ _ _

He Was a Beast About Beauty

He hated every girl he dated;
He couldn't find a one that rated.
He raved in dreams of perfect mates,
And roved the earth for candidates,
Yet loved none. (He was double-gaited.)

H A T E D
R A T E D
R A V E D
R O V E D
L O V E D

The Poor Girl Could Not Look Him in the Eye

The _ _ _ _ _ of the serpent in Eden was _ _ _ _ _,
For he knew that he _ _ _ _ _, which of course was no fun.
Since the _ _ _ _ _ of a serpent grows worse after dark,
He'd _ _ _ _ _ off each day at the set of the sun.
Come morn, though, his ego he'd salve in a wink
By staring Eve down, since a snake cannot _ _ _ _ _.

_ _ _ _ _
_ _ _ _ _
_ _ _ _ _
_ _ _ _ _
_ _ _ _ _
_ _ _ _ _

The Poor Girl Could Not Look Him in the Eye

The stare of the serpent in Eden was stark,
For he knew that he stank, which of course was no fun.
Since the stink of a serpent grows worse after dark,
He'd slink off each day at the set of the sun.
Come morn, though, his ego he'd salve in a wink
By staring Eve down, since a snake cannot blink.

S T A R E
S T A R K
S T A N K
S T I N K
S L I N K
B L I N K

There's Plenty More Fish in the Sea

A salmon's _ _ _ _ _ belly gleams out of the fjord;
I hear the winch _ _ _ _ _ as it hauls him aboard.
I'd _ _ _ _ _ him for supper, but first I must look
For a _ _ _ _ _ in the heart of the _ _ _ _ _ who's the cook.
She'll _ _ _ _ _ and she'll _ _ _ _ _ and refuse me my wish,
For she's _ _ _ _ _ in her soul, and as cold as the fish.

_ _ _ _ _
_ _ _ _ _
_ _ _ _ _
_ _ _ _ _
_ _ _ _ _
_ _ _ _ _
_ _ _ _ _
_ _ _ _ _

There's Plenty More Fish in the Sea

A salmon's white belly gleams out of the fjord;
I hear the winch whine as it hauls him aboard.
I'd chine him for supper, but first I must look
For a chink in the heart of the chick who's the cook.
She'll click and she'll clack and refuse me my wish,
For she's black in her soul, and as cold as the fish.


```
W H I T E
W H I N E
C H I N E
C H I N K
C H I C K
C L I C K
C L A C K
B L A C K
```

No More Doch-an-Dorris for Poor Jock

Jock MacIntosh, who from his _ _ _ _ _
Did by a _ _ _ _ _ reside,
Set _ _ _ _ _ one day to prove his worth
And stormed the _ _ _ _ _ of Clyde.
A lawyer, who of _ _ _ _ _ knew more
Than Jock e'en knew of _ _ _ _ _
Declared the act unjustified,
And hanged him in his _ _ _ _ _.
Ah, boats still _ _ _ _ _ the ocean's teeth;
The sea still _ _ _ _ _ the rock;
The summer sun still _ _ _ _ _ the _ _ _ _ _,
But _ _ _ _ _ has come to Jock.

_ _ _ _ _
_ _ _ _ _
_ _ _ _ _
_ _ _ _ _
_ _ _ _ _
_ _ _ _ _
_ _ _ _ _
_ _ _ _ _
_ _ _ _ _
_ _ _ _ _
_ _ _ _ _
_ _ _ _ _

No More Doch-an-Dorris for Poor Jock

Jock MacIntosh, who from his birth
Did by a firth reside,
Set forth one day to prove his worth
And stormed the forts of Clyde.
A lawyer, who of torts knew more
Than Jock e'en knew of toots,
Declared the act unjustified,
And hanged him in his boots.
Ah, boats still brave the ocean's teeth;
The sea still beats the rock;
The summer sun still heats the heath,
But death has come to Jock.

B I R T H
F I R T H
F O R T H
F O R T S
T O R T S
T O O T S
B O O T S
B O A T S
B E A T S
H E A T S
H E A T H
D E A T H

The Salutary Fable of the Weasel and the Oyster

A _ _ _ _ _ Aegean weasel once was drawn by sense
   of _ _ _ _ _
To raid an Attic cottage, where an oyster in its _ _ _ _ _ _
(Or, better, carapace) sat high upon a kitchen _ _ _ _ _
Beside a _ _ _ _ _ of barley. There the oyster sunned itself.
The weasel, though the carapace was much too tough
   to _ _ _ _ _,
Knew _ _ _ _ _ delight of oyster flesh would bring its
   belly _ _ _ _ _.
And so it told the oyster, "Sir, forgive a bit of _ _ _ _ _,
But I think you'd have to open if I dropped you in
   the _ _ _ _ _."
The oyster answered, "I am _ _ _ _ _, my friend, and so
   are you.
Let's _ _ _ _ _ _ _ _ _ _ Zeus as countrymen; don't
   make me oyster stew."

— — — — —
— — — — —
— — — — —
— — — — —
— — — — —
— — — — —
— — — — —
— — — — —
— — — — —
— — — — —
— — — — —
— — — — —
— — — — —

The Salutary Fable of the Weasel and the Oyster

A small Aegean weasel once was drawn by sense of smell
To raid an Attic cottage, where an oyster in its shell
(Or, better, carapace) sat high upon a kitchen shelf
Beside a sheaf of barley. There the oyster sunned itself.
The weasel, though the carapace was much too tough to shear,
Knew sheer delight of oyster flesh would bring its belly cheer.
And so it told the oyster, "Sir, forgive a bit of cheek,
But I think you'd have to open if I dropped you in the creek."
The oyster answered, "I am Greek, my friend, and so are you.
Let's greet great Zeus as countrymen; don't make me oyster stew."

S M A L L
S M E L L
S H E L L
S H E L F
S H E A F
S H E A R
S H E E R
C H E E R
C R E E K
C H E E K
G R E E K
G R E E T
G R E A T

Too Bad — Virtue Sometimes Fails to Triumph

"Say why do you _ _ _ _ _ so, dear captain, and pause?
Many missions ere this one we've _ _ _ _ _.
The Rhine _ _ _ _ _ beneath us; we'll catch Jerry's _ _ _ _ _
Here as well as we did on the Rhone.
The _ _ _ _ ' _ a bit heavy, but needn't affright;
Not a _ _ _ _ _ will come near us, I trust.
Our blood lust we'll _ _ _ _ _ upon Jerry tonight;
We'll crush that _ _ _ _ _ into the dust."
So _ _ _ _ _ the co-pilot, attempting to _ _ _ _ _
His captain's forebodings — but O!
In _ _ _ _ _ of the comforting, Jerry did _ _ _ _ _;
Now the _ _ _ _ _'s on the face of the foe.

_ _ _ _ _
_ _ _ _ _
_ _ _ _ _
_ _ _ _ _, _
_ _ _ _ ' _
_ _ _ _ _
_ _ _ _ _
_ _ _ _ _
_ _ _ _ _
_ _ _ _ _
_ _ _ _ _
_ _ _ _ _
_ _ _ _ _

· 89 ·

Too Bad—Virtue Sometimes Fails to Triumph

"Say why do you frown so, dear captain, and pause?
Many missions ere this one we've flown.
The Rhine flows beneath us; we'll catch Jerry's flaws
Here as well as we did on the Rhone.
The flak's a bit heavy, but needn't affright;
Not a flake will come near us, I trust.
Our blood lust we'll slake upon Jerry tonight;
We'll crush that snake into the dust."
So spake the co-pilot, attempting to spike
His captain's forebodings—but O!
In spite of the comforting, Jerry did smite;
Now the smile's on the face of the foe.

```
F R O W N
F L O W N
F L O W S
F L A W S
F L A K' S
F L A K E
S L A K E
S N A K E
S P A K E
S P I K E
S P I T E
S M I T E
S M I L E
```

And Quite Right; He Didn't Lift a Finger

The _ _ _ _ _ has fallen in the _ _ _ _ _!
She's on the _ _ _ _ _ of dying!
But in a _ _ _ _ _ young Ballantine
(Who's _ _ _ _ _ of brain and prone to pine
And _ _ _ _ _ of face and full of wine)
His fate with hers will _ _ _ _ _ (align)—
Or _ _ _ _ _ and die a-trying.
The Ballantines, a wealthy _ _ _ _ _,
Have buttered _ _ _ _ _ to live on;
Their lands are _ _ _ _ _, and men in need
Oft _ _ _ _ _ on how they've thriven.
B. saves the bride; she takes a _ _ _ _ _
And pummels the unhappy _ _ _ _ _.

_ _ _ _ _
_ _ _ _ _
_ _ _ _ _
_ _ _ _ _
_ _ _ _ _
_ _ _ _ _
_ _ _ _ _
_ _ _ _ _
_ _ _ _ _
_ _ _ _ _
_ _ _ _ _
_ _ _ _ _
_ _ _ _ _
_ _ _ _ _

And Quite Right; He Didn't Lift a Finger

The bride has fallen in the brine!
She's on the brink of dying!
But in a blink young Ballantine
(Who's blank of brain and prone to pine
And bland of face and full of wine)
His fate with hers will blend (align)—
Or bleed and die a-trying.
The Ballantines, a wealthy breed,
Have buttered bread to live on;
Their lands are broad, and men in need
Oft brood on how they've thriven.
B. saves the bride; she takes a broom
And pummels the unhappy groom.

```
B R I D E
B R I N E
B R I N K
B L I N K
B L A N K
B L A N D
B L E N D
B L E E D
B R E E D
B R E A D
B R O A D
B R O O D
B R O O M
G R O O M
```

BRIDE   *BRIDE*
PRIDE
PRIZE   *BRINE*

Wake Up, Cy—Time to Milk the Chickens!

The farm's in _ _ _ _ _, Cy. Who moults?
The sheep! Who _ _ _ _ _? The cow! Who makes
Fur _ _ _ _ _? The duck! Who for? The _ _ _ _ _!
Who swims? The speckled hen! Who _ _ _ _ _
The barn door shut? The kitten, for gosh' sake!

Who lines his nest with tree _ _ _ _ _? Why,
The goat! Cy, tell me what this _ _ _ _ _:
The goose _ _ _ _ _ in the old pig's sty!
Who's that _ _ _ _ _ off and waves good-bye?
The _ _ _ _ _'s Fido, standing on two toads!

Cy, can't you help? No _ _ _ _ _'s nigh—
An _ _ _ _ _'s in the cornfield sowing;
Still _ _ _ _ _, snails are rushing by,
And stand not on the _ _ _ _ _ of their going.

_ _ _ _ _
_ _ _ _ _
_ _ _ _ _
_ _ _ _ _
_ _ _ _ _
_ _ _ _ _
_ _ _ _ _
_ _ _ _ _
_ _ _ _ _
_ _ _ _ _
_ _ _ _ _
_ _ _ _ _
_ _ _ _ _
_ _ _ _ _

Wake Up, Cy—Time to Milk the Chickens!

The farm's in chaos, Cy. Who moults?
The sheep! Who chats? The cow! Who makes
Fur coats? The duck! Who for? The colts!
Who swims? The speckled hen! Who bolts
The barn door shut? The kitten, for gosh' sake!

Who lines his nest with tree boles? Why,
The goat! Cy, tell me what this bodes:
The goose bides in the old pig's sty!
Who's that rides off and waves good-bye?
The rider's Fido, standing on two toads!

Cy, can't you help? No aider's nigh—
An adder's in the cornfield sowing;
Still odder, snails are rushing by,
And stand not on the order of their going.

C H A O S
C H A T S
C O A T S
C O L T S
B O L T S
B O L E S
B O D E S
B I D E S
R I D E S
R I D E R
A I D E R
A D D E R
O D D E R
O R D E R

They Might Try Bundling

_ _ _ _ _ _ is the time to _ _ _ _ _ _,
Time to watch the dusk grow _ _ _ _ _ _;
When it's _ _ _ _ _ _ to firefly glow,
Time to let _ _ _ _ _ _ passion flow.
Kisses' fires aren't _ _ _ _ _ _ by sweat;
_ _ _ _ _ _ hugs are sweeter yet.
No. To _ _ _ _ _ _ love, to still
Sound of _ _ _ _ _ _ on the hill,
Needs a season _ _ _ _ _ _, colder;
Needs a _ _ _ _ _ _ dourer, older.
Them who _ _ _ _ _ _ in embrace
_ _ _ _ _ _ days will soon unlace.
Love's the _ _ _ _ _ _, till it's chilly;
In the _ _ _ _ _ _, it seems silly.

_ _ _ _ _ _
_ _ _ _ _ _
_ _ _ _ _ _
_ _ _ _ _ _
_ _ _ _ _ _
_ _ _ _ _ _
_ _ _ _ _ _
_ _ _ _ _ _
_ _ _ _ _ _
_ _ _ _ _ _
_ _ _ _ _ _
_ _ _ _ _ _
_ _ _ _ _ _

They Might Try Bundling

Summer is the time to simmer,
Time to watch the dusk grow dimmer;
When it's dimmed to firefly glow,
Time to let dammed passion flow.
Kisses' fires aren't damped by sweat;
Damper hugs are sweeter yet.
No. To hamper love, to still
Sound of harper on the hill,
Needs a season harder, colder;
Needs a warden dourer, older.
Them who wander in embrace
Wanner days will soon unlace.
Love's the winner, till it's chilly;
In the winter, it seems silly.

S U M M E R
S I M M E R
D I M M E R
D I M M E D
D A M M E D
D A M P E D
D A M P E R
H A M P E R
H A R P E R
H A R D E R
W A R D E R
W A N D E R
W A N N E R
W I N N E R
W I N T E R

ESPYramids

The missing words are anagrams of each other, except that a letter is added in each succeeding word. (Many of the puzzles are in the form of inverted pyramids. In these, a letter is *subtracted* in each succeeding word.)

Below each verse/puzzle is a space, especially designed for that puzzle, in which to work out your solutions. (For this first ESPYramid you may not need it, but the work spaces may come in handy for the longer and more challenging puzzles ahead.)

It's All My Own Fault

_, it will sadden you _ _ know
I've _ _ _ the _ _ _ _ in my great toe.
_ _ _ _ _ luck, but not surprising, _ _ _ _ _ _
I never _ _ _ _ _ _ _ 'twould hurt me so.

—
— —
— — —
— — — —
— — — — —
— — — — — —
— — — — — — —

Want help?
Turn to page 187 for clues to the longest missing word.

It's All My Own Fault

O, it will sadden you to know
I've got the gout in my great toe.
Tough luck, but not surprising, though
I never thought 'twould hurt me so.

O
TO
GOT
GOUT
TOUGH
THOUGH
THOUGHT

And Think of All the Chances He Has!

Why does the great _ _ _ _ _ _ _ _ _ _ _ _ _
To keep his virtue free of _ _ _ _ _?
It _ _ _'_ that he hates to _ _ _,
But that he holds his passions _ _.
This doubtless saves his soul from hell.
Why is it _ can't do as well?

_ _ _ _ _ _ _
_ _ _ _ _ _ _
_ _ _ _ _ _
_ _ _'_
_ _ _
_ _
_

Want help?
Turn to page 187 for clues to the longest missing word.

And Think of All the Chances He Has!

Why does the great Sinatra strain
To keep his virtue free of stain?
It isn't that he hates to sin,
But that he holds his passions in.
This doubtless saves his soul from hell.
Why is it I can't do as well?

S I N A T R A
S T R A I N
S T A I N
I S N'T
S I N
I N
I

When He Went Off His Diet, He Overdid It

_ hungry man _ _ lunch went wild,
And _ _ _ his mother, wife, and child.
At dinner on the self-same _ _ _ _,
Not _ _ _ _ _ yet, his pa he ate.
Cops found him _ _ _ _ _ _, still at sup,
_ _ _ _ _ _ _ him, and locked him up.

—
— —
— — —
— — — —
— — — — —
— — — — — —
— — — — — — —

Want help?
Turn to page 187 for clues to the longest missing word.

When He Went Off His Diet, He Overdid It

A hungry man at lunch went wild,
And ate his mother, wife, and child.
At dinner on the self-same date,
Not sated yet, his pa he ate.
Cops found him seated, still at sup,
Sedated him, and locked him up.

A
AT
ATE
DATE
SATED
SEATED
SEDATED

Good Night, Good Knight

A knight at _ _ _ _ _ _ _, hurt in courtly fray,
His _ _ _ _ _ _ untended, wobbling on his mare,
In deep'ning gloaming _ _ _ _ _ his woeful way,
Till tumbling _ _ _ _ he murmured, dying there,
" _ _ _ falls the night, and falls the knight; _ _ one
Ere me, _ Lord, has perished for a pun."

_ _ _ _ _ _ _
_ _ _ _ _ _
_ _ _ _ _
_ _ _ _
_ _ _
_ _
_

Want help?
Turn to page 187 for clues to the longest missing word.

Good Night, Good Knight

A knight at sundown, hurt in courtly fray,
His wounds untended, wobbling on his mare,
In deep'ning gloaming wound his woeful way,
Till tumbling down he murmured, dying there,
"Now falls the night, and falls the knight; no one
Ere me, O Lord, has perished for a pun."

SUNDOWN
WOUNDS
WOUND
DOWN
NOW
NO
O

And You're Not Perfect, Either

True, I'm _ _ _ _ _ _ _ _ silly verse—
_ _ _ _ _ _ _ sense for something worse;
The _ _ _ _ _ _ of my lines is nil;
My _ _ _ _ _ of thought is niller still.
True, my follies make you _ _ _ _;
True, I'm cricket to your _ _ _;
True, _ _ idle sort's what I'm—
Still, I have _ jolly time.

_ _ _ _ _ _ _ _
_ _ _ _ _ _ _
_ _ _ _ _ _
_ _ _ _ _
_ _ _ _
_ _ _
_ _
_

Want help?
Turn to page 187 for clues to the longest missing word.

And You're Not Perfect, Either

True, I'm drafting silly verse—
Trading sense for something worse;
The rating of my lines is nil;
My train of thought is niller still.
True, my follies make you rant;
True, I'm cricket to your ant;
True, an idle sort's what I'm—
Still, I have a jolly time.

DRAFTING
TRADING
RATING
TRAIN
RANT
ANT
AN
A

He Was Finally Expelled

— high school boy would not _ _ good be
As friends and teachers thought he should be.
Though threatened with a rod of _ _ _,
He made off with the petty _ _ _ _.
He loved to _ _ _ _ _ the girls, and if
One turned out _ _ _ _ _ _, would sneer and sniff.
This _ _ _ _ _ _ _ us that even schools
Cannot cure _ _ _ _ _ _ _ _, thieves, and fools.

—
— —
— — —
— — — —
— — — — —
— — — — — —
— — — — — — —
— — — — — — — —

Want help?

Turn to page 187 for clues to the longest missing word.

He Was Finally Expelled

A high school boy would not as good be
As friends and teachers thought he should be.
Though threatened with a rod of ash,
He made off with the petty cash.
He loved to chase the girls, and if
One turned out chaste, would sneer and sniff.
This teaches us that even schools
Cannot cure cheaters, thieves, and fools.

A
A S
A S H
C A S H
C H A S E
C H A S T E
T E A C H E S
C H E A T E R S

It's Worth Considering These Nuclear Days

A priestly _ _ _ _ _ _ _ _ along the Nile
To honor the god Ra with _ _ _ _ _ _ _ and such
Miscarried; to _ _ _ _ _ _ was more worthwhile,
The fellaheen declared. (They don't _ _ _ _ _ much.)
They changed it to a love feast, free of _ _ _ _;
If myths _ _ _ true, _ _ downed _ flagon there.

_ _ _ _ _ _ _ _
_ _ _ _ _ _ _
_ _ _ _ _ _
_ _ _ _ _
_ _ _ _
_ _ _
_ _
_

Want help?

Turn to page 187 for clues to the longest missing word.

It's Worth Considering These Nuclear Days

A priestly massacre along the Nile
To honor the god Ra with screams and such
Miscarried; to caress was more worthwhile,
The fellaheen declared. (They don't scare much.)
They changed it to a love feast, free of care;
If myths are true, Ra downed a flagon there.

MASSACRE
SCREAMS
CARESS
SCARE
CARE
ARE
RA
A

Faith Rewarded

_ sailor, _ _ he set to _ _ _
To bring back _ _ _ _ from Barbary,
Prayed, "Father, _ _ _ _ _ me, and I swear
I'll _ _ _ _ _ _ _ Thy glory everywhere!"
He _ _ _ _ _ _ _ the Lord, nor felt surprise*
To wake next morn in _ _ _ _ _ _ _ _.

*Change "nor felt surprise" to "and found it nice" for the rhyme if you prefer the alternative pronunciation of the final missing word.

—
— —
— — —
— — — —
— — — — —
— — — — — —
— — — — — — —
— — — — — — — —

Want help?

Turn to page 187 for clues to the longest missing word.

Faith Rewarded

A sailor, as he set to sea
To bring back apes from Barbary,
Prayed, "Father, spare me, and I swear
I'll spread Thy glory everywhere!"
He praised the Lord, nor felt surprise
To wake next morn in Paradise.

A
A S
S E A
A P E S
S P A R E
S P R E A D
P R A I S E D
P A R A D I S E

I Remember When You Did the Same, Dear

With men our daughter _ _ _ _ _ _ _ _ out;
At _ _ _ _ _ _ _ she meets others.
She _ _ _ _ _ _ of some she's wild about,
And then she _ _ _ _ _ their brothers.
No _ _ _ _ of female _ _ _ is guessed—
It's sucked in _ _   _ mother's breast.

_ _ _ _ _ _ _ _
_ _ _ _ _ _ _
_ _ _ _ _ _
_ _ _ _ _
_ _ _ _
_ _ _
_ _
_

Want help?
Turn to page 187 for clues to the longest missing word.

I Remember When You Did the Same, Dear

With men our daughter traipses out;
At parties she meets others.
She prates of some she's wild about,
And then she traps their brothers.
No part of female art is guessed—
It's sucked in at a mother's breast.


```
TRAIPSES
PARTIES
PRATES
TRAPS
PART
ART
AT
A
```

Frankly, I'd Prefer a Rocking Horse

_ deem _ _ useful, if perforce
Some day I have to _ _ _ a horse,
To find a _ _ _ _ on which to fall
For final _ _ _ _ _ and burial.
My _ _ _ _ _ _ terror, I confide,
Would be to fall off when _ _ _ _ _ _ _
Some bucking beast, and die unblessed:
The soul forewarned is _ _ _ _ _ _ _ _.

_
_ _
_ _ _
_ _ _ _
_ _ _ _ _
_ _ _ _ _ _
_ _ _ _ _ _ _
_ _ _ _ _ _ _ _

Want help?
Turn to page 187 for clues to the longest missing word.

Frankly, I'd Prefer a Rocking Horse

I deem it useful, if perforce
Some day I have to sit a horse,
To find a site on which to fall
For final rites and burial.
My direst terror, I confide,
Would be to fall off when astride
Some bucking beast, and die unblessed:
The soul forewarned is readiest.

```
I
IT
SIT
SITE
RITES
DIREST
ASTRIDE
READIEST
```

Unlikely Litany

Upon his tomb this legend is _ _ _ _ _ _ _ _
" _ _ _ _ _ _ he of man and maid enslaved."
Perched on the _ _ _ _ _ _ stone a _ _ _ _ _ stares;
Above, a weather _ _ _ _ records the airs.
A nearby _ _ _ displays _ _ argent crest—
As sensible _ sight as all the rest.

_ _ _ _ _ _ _ _
_ _ _ _ _ _ _
_ _ _ _ _ _
_ _ _ _ _
_ _ _ _
_ _ _
_ _
_

Want help?
Turn to page 187 for clues to the longest missing word.

Unlikely Litany

Upon his tomb this legend is engraved:
"Avenger he of man and maid enslaved."
Perched on the graven stone a raven stares;
Above, a weather vane records the airs.
A nearby van displays an argent crest—
As sensible a sight as all the rest.

E N G R A V E D
A V E N G E R
G R A V E N
R A V E N
V A N E
V A N
A N
A

He Should Have Counted to Ten First

— man names Tim espied an _ _
That vilified the _._._.*
He raged, "How _ _ _ _ they? It's too bad!
Who _ _ _ _ _ such stuff? This goes too far!"

Crowds gathered 'round and _ _ _ _ _ _ at him;
These too he _ _ _ _ _ _ _ _, till, annoyed,
They bought a rocket, stuck in Tim,
And sent him to an _ _ _ _ _ _ _ _.

*An organization of patriotic women.

—
— —
—. —. —.
— — — —
— — — — —
— — — — — —
— — — — — — —
— — — — — — — —

Want help?
Turn to page 187 for clues to the longest missing word.

He Should Have Counted to Ten First

A man names Tim espied an ad
That vilified the D.A.R.
He raged, "How dare they? It's too bad!
Who reads such stuff? This goes too far!"

Crowds gathered 'round and stared at him;
These too he roasted, till, annoyed,
They bought a rocket, stuck in Tim,
And sent him to an asteroid.

A
A D
D.A.R.
D A R E
R E A D S
S T A R E D
R O A S T E D
A S T E R O I D

The U.N. Wouldn't Permit It Nowadays

When Captain _ _ _ _ _ _ _ _ sailed the sea
His _ _ _ _ _ _ _ were filled with jealousy;
For "_ _ _ _ _ _ keeper!" he would cry
As each new isle he scudded by;
And I _ _ _ _ _ from what I read
The isles he kept were _ _ _ _ indeed.
(Do I hear "_ _ _!"? _ _ you could do
The same, you would, and _ would too.)

(But the fact is that though the captain explored New South Wales, circumnavigated Tasmania, and surveyed the west coast of Australia, he kept nothing for himself; he turned over the islands to good King George.)

— — — — — — — —
— — — — — — —
— — — — — —
— — — — —
— — — —
— — —
— —
—

Want help?
Turn to page 187 for clues to the longest missing word.

The U.N. Wouldn't Permit It Nowadays

When Captain Flinders sailed the sea
His friends were filled with jealousy;
For "Finder keeper!" he would cry
As each new isle he scudded by;
And I infer from what I read
The isles he kept were fine indeed.
(Do I hear "Fie!"? If you could do
The same, you would, and I would too.)

FLINDERS
FRIENDS
FINDER
INFER
FINE
FIE
IF
I

But I Suppose They Do Have Fun Sometimes

_ _ _ _ _ _ _ jeer at _ _ _ _ _ _ folk;
_ _ _ _ _ _ make chastity a joke—
Move in _ _ _ _ _ from mate to mate,
Love today, tomorrow _ _ _ _;
Tip their _ _ _ and move along,
Puzzling _ _ _ life gone wrong.

— — — — — — — —
— — — — — — —
— — — — — —
— — — — —
— — — —
— — —
— —
—

Want help?
Turn to page 187 for clues to the longest missing word.

But I Suppose They Do Have Fun Sometimes

Cheaters jeer at chaster folk;
Cheats make chastity a joke—
Move in haste from mate to mate,
Love today, tomorrow hate;
Tip their hat and move along,
Puzzling at a life gone wrong.

CHEATERS
CHASTER
CHEATS
HASTE
HATE
HAT
AT
A

A
AT
HAT
HEAT
HEATS
CHEATS

He Wasn't for Sale, Though

— tattered wino — — a — — — sale whined
"I crashed the — — — — to see what I might find.
Although your — — — — — holds junk—old — — — — — —
     and chairs
At prices that would — — — — — — — millionaires,
I'm — — — — — — — — of all the junky kind."

—
— —
— — —
— — — —
— — — — —
— — — — — —
— — — — — — —
— — — — — — — —

Want help?
Turn to page 187 for clues to the longest missing word.

He Wasn't for Sale, Though

A tattered wino at a tag sale whined
"I crashed the gate to see what I might find.
Although your stage holds junk—old grates and chairs
At prices that would stagger millionaires,
I'm raggiest of all the junky kind."

A
AT
TAG
GATE
STAGE
GRATES
STAGGER
RAGGIEST

Chance Spins the Wheel

The _ _ _ _ _ _ _ _ of a life perhaps
Begin with _ _ _ _ _ _ _; yet I vow
A good _ _ _ _ _ _ has altered chaps,
And _ _ _ _ _ that paled a woman's brow
Has led _ _ _ _ empires to collapse.
The _ _ _ at Cleopatra's throat
_ _ willingly had slain _ goat.

_ _ _ _ _ _ _ _
_ _ _ _ _ _ _
_ _ _ _ _ _
_ _ _ _ _
_ _ _ _
_ _ _
_ _
_

Want help?
Turn to page 187 for clues to the longest missing word.

Chance Spins the Wheel

The patterns of a life perhaps
Begin with parents; yet I vow
A good repast has altered chaps,
And paste that paled a woman's brow
Has led past empires to collapse.
The asp at Cleopatra's throat
As willingly had slain a goat.

PATTERNS
PARENTS
REPAST
PASTE
PAST
ASP
AS
A

And They're Smooth Going Down

_ fool _ _ dinner would not _ _ _.
He said, "Of _ _ _ _ I like food sweet.
Please _ _ _ _ _ what you serve to me;
I best _ _ _ _ _ _ to sugared tea
And _ _ _ _ _ _ _. They are cloying, but
They do not _ _ _ _ _ _ _ _ the gut."

_
_ _
_ _ _
_ _ _ _
_ _ _ _ _
_ _ _ _ _ _
_ _ _ _ _ _ _
_ _ _ _ _ _ _ _

Want help?
Turn to page 187 for clues to the longest missing word.

And They're Smooth Going Down

A fool at dinner would not eat.
He said, "Of late I like food sweet.
Please alter what you serve to me;
I best relate to sugared tea
And treacle. They are cloying, but
They do not lacerate the gut."

A
AT
EAT
LATE
ALTER
RELATE
TREACLE
LACERATE

We Both Go to Bed Hungry

The farmer won't his _ _ _ _ _ _ _ _ stem;
He _ _ _ _ _ _ _ more than half of them;
He _ _ _ _ _ _ his sheep—the wool's forgot;
The _ _ _ _ _ he traps he leaves to rot;
He raises corn to _ _ _ _ _* it; he
Throws milk and sugar in the _ _ _,
And _ _   _ rule leaves none for me.

*This is a variant spelling.

_ _ _ _ _ _ _ _
_ _ _ _ _ _ _
_ _ _ _ _ _
_ _ _ _ _
_ _ _ _
_ _ _
_ _
_

Want help?
Turn to page 187 for clues to the longest missing word.

We Both Go to Bed Hungry

The farmer won't his harvests stem;
He trashes more than half of them;
He shears his sheep — the wool's forgot;
The hares he traps he leaves to rot;
He raises corn to rase it; he
Throws milk and sugar in the sea,
And as a rule leaves none for me.

HARVESTS
TRASHES
SHEARS ✓
HARES ~~RASES~~ SHEAR
RASE SEAR
SEA
AS
A

There's Gold in Them Sandlots

When _ _ _ _ _ _ _ baseball players, or
When _ _ _ _ _ _ _ them about,
Their _ _ _ _ _ _ has to meet a score
Of questions from the scout.
Like, Is he hard to _ _ _ _ _? And, Can
He hit as well as steal?
And, Would he _ _ _ _ if he should fan?
And, Is his _ _ _ for real?
(_ _ first this may seem picky, but
_ million dollars is the nut.)

_ _ _ _ _ _ _ _
_ _ _ _ _ _ _
_ _ _ _ _ _
_ _ _ _ _
_ _ _ _
_ _ _
_ _
_

Want help?
Turn to page 187 for clues to the longest missing word.

There's Gold in Them Sandlots

When drafting baseball players, or
When trading them about,
Their rating has to meet a score
Of questions from the scout.
Like, Is he hard to train? And, Can
He hit as well as steal?
And, Would he rant if he should fan?
And, Is his tan for real?
(At first this may seem picky, but
A million dollars is the nut.)

DRAFTING
TRADING
RATING
TRAIN
RANT
TAN
AT
A

Schizophrenia, No Doubt

_ worm once in _ _ apple grew;
An old _ _ _ bit the worm in two,
A _ _ _ _ and naughty thing to do.
The two halves _ _ _ _ _ him in a suit;
They made _ _ _ _ _ _ he restitute
Their former state inside the fruit.
Their fate could not _ _ _ _ _ _ _ be,
Which _ _ _ _ _ _ _ _ them, as it would me.

_
_ _
_ _ _
_ _ _ _
_ _ _ _ _
_ _ _ _ _ _
_ _ _ _ _ _ _
_ _ _ _ _ _ _ _

Want help?
Turn to page 187 for clues to the longest missing word.

Schizophrenia, No Doubt

A worm once in an apple grew;
An old man bit the worm in two,
A mean and naughty thing to do.
The two halves named him in a suit;
They made demand he restitute
Their former state inside the fruit.
Their fate could not amended be,
Which maddened them, as it would me.

A
AN
MAN
MEAN   MANE
NAMED ✓
DEMAND
AMENDED
MADDENED

How *Can* You Do Worse?

Jack, seldom _ _ _ _ _ _ _ _ with wit,
_ _ _ _ _ _ _ rhymes that didn't fit,
Yet seized the _ _ _ _ _ _ in a _ _ _ _ _.
Said he, "I _ _ _ _ you this advice:
If you this verse can't beat or _ _ _,
_ _ means you scribble worse than _."

_ _ _ _ _ _ _ _
_ _ _ _ _ _ _
_ _ _ _ _ _
_ _ _ _ _
_ _ _ _
_ _ _
_ _
_

Want help?
Turn to page 187 for clues to the longest missing word.

How *Can* You Do Worse?

Jack, seldom credited with wit,
Recited rhymes that didn't fit,
Yet seized the credit in a trice.
Said he, "I cite you this advice:
If you this verse can't beat or tie,
It means you scribble worse than I."

CREDITED
RECITED
CREDIT
TRICE
CITE
TIE
IT
I

Perhaps We Need More Idlers Like That

Why waste our time on _ _ _ _ _ _ _ _' silliness,
When we have _ _ _ _ _ _ _ that could screen them out?
With life _ _ _ _ _ _ so brief, why let them press
Their frolics on us? . . . Well, each _ _ _ _ _ about,
Tells here some joke, gives there some heart a _ _ _ _ _.
(A fit employ! _ _ _ but had that gift . . .)

_ _ _ _ _ _ _ _
_ _ _ _ _ _ _
_ _ _ _ _ _
_ _ _ _ _
_ _ _ _
_ _ _
_ _
_

Want help?
Turn to page 187 for clues to the longest missing word.

Perhaps We Need More Idlers Like That

Why waste our time on triflers' silliness,
When we have filters that could screen them out?
With life itself so brief, why let them press
Their frolics on us?... Well, each flits about,
Tells here some joke, gives there some heart a lift.
(A fit employ! If I but had that gift...)

TRIFLERS
FILTERS
ITSELF
FLITS
LIFT
FIT
IF
I

I Can't Even Get Into the Saddle

In sore _ _ _ _ _ _ _ _ the poet _ _ _ _ _ _ _;
In direst dread he mounts and _ _ _ _ _
Great Pegasus, to _ _ _ _ whom most
Would gladly _ _ _ (give up the ghost).
Don't say you're sorry for him! _'_
Give all if _ could share that ride.

_ _ _ _ _ _ _ _
_ _ _ _ _ _ _
_ _ _ _ _ _
_ _ _ _ _
_ _ _ _
_ _'_ _
_'_
_

Want help?
Turn to page 187 for clues to the longest missing word.

I Can't Even Get Into the Saddle

In sore distress the poet strides;
In direst dread he mounts and rides
Great Pegasus, to ride whom most
Would gladly die (give up the ghost).
Don't say you're sorry for him! I'd
Give all if I could share that ride.

DISTRESS
STRIDES
DIREST
RIDES
RIDE
DIE
I'D
I

Envy at Eighty

_ _ _ be young again: puffing on _ _ _,
Putting the wicked old world on the _ _ _ _,
Gloomy as _ _ _ _ _ and drinking like _ _ _ _ _ _,
Quick at _ _ _ _ _ _ _ and impatient of hopers!
Once we were _ _ _ _ _ _ _ _. Nobody cares
That we have stopped kissing behind the _ _ _ _ _ _ _ _ _.

_
_ _
_ _ _
_ _ _ _
_ _ _ _ _
_ _ _ _ _ _
_ _ _ _ _ _ _
_ _ _ _ _ _ _ _
_ _ _ _ _ _ _ _ _

Want help?
Turn to page 187 for clues to the longest missing word.

Envy at Eighty

O to be young again: puffing on pot,
Putting the wicked old world on the spot,
Gloomy as poets and drinking like topers,
Quick at riposte and impatient of hopers!
Once we were sportier. Nobody cares
That we have stopped kissing behind the portieres.

O
TO
POT
SPOT
POETS — *SPORT*
TOPERS — *TOTERS*
RIPOSTE *RIPOSTE*
SPORTIER
PORTIERES

The Word Does Mean Christian, You Know

Perhaps _ _ _ _ _ _ _ _'_ not as bad
As your _ _ _ _ _ _ _ _ would suppose;
The smartest _ _ _ _ _ _ _ my lad,
May miss the truth the _ _ _ _ _ _ knows.
When men _ _ _ _ _ you, though your _ _ _ _
Be grave with prayers and rich with jewels,
Your _ _ _ with God may turn out slight;
_ _ won't, _ think, outmatch the fool's.

_ _ _ _ _ _ _ _' _
_ _ _ _ _ _ _ _
_ _ _ _ _ _ _
_ _ _ _ _ _
_ _ _ _ _
_ _ _ _
_ _ _
_ _
_

Want help?
Turn to page 187 for clues to the longest missing word.

The Word Does Mean Christian, You Know

Perhaps Creation's not as bad
As your reaction would suppose;
The smartest noticer, my lad,
May miss the truth the cretin knows.
When men inter you, though your rite
Be grave with prayers and rich with jewels,
Your tie with God may turn out slight;
It won't, I think, outmatch the fool's.

CREATION'S
REACTION
NOTICER
CRETIN
INTER
RITE
TIE
IT
I

I Didn't Know Bedouins Wore Them

_ Bedouin built _ _ igloo
(As Bedouins frequently do),
And arranged, before taking his _ _ _,
In several _ _ _ _ to entrap
The drip from the ice, which perchance
Might otherwise ruin his _ _ _ _ _.
The drip thus collected he'd use
To make his _ _ _ _ _ _ green and profuse.
(To _ _ _ _ _ _ _ that gazed on his roof
These crops were the _ _ _ _ _ _ _ _ of proof
That a Bedouin might, if he chose,
Make _ _ _ _ _ _ _ _ _ bloom like a rose.)

—
— —
— — —
— — — —
— — — — —
— — — — — —
— — — — — — —
— — — — — — — —
— — — — — — — — —

Want help?
Turn to page 187 for clues to the longest missing word.

· 147 ·

I Didn't Know Bedouins Wore Them

A Bedouin built an igloo
(As Bedouins frequently do),
And arranged, before taking his nap,
In several pans to entrap
The drip from the ice, which perchance
Might otherwise ruin his pants.
The drip thus collected he'd use
To make his plants green and profuse.
(To planets that gazed on his roof
These crops were the plainest of proof
That a Bedouin might, if he chose,
Make Palestine bloom like a rose.)

A
AN
NAP
PANS
PANTS
PLANTS
PLANETS
PLAINEST
PALESTINE

O Say Can You See?... Well, Not Often

The Eagle _ _ _ _ _ _ _ _ _, while my son
In _ _ _ _ _ _ _ _ uniform has fun.
He _ _ _ _ _ _ _ to the dame he's hot on,
And _ _ _ _ _ _ her with the duds he's got on—
Yet _ _ _ _ _ her not, nor mars her virtue;
He says, "_ _'_ right; I mustn't hurt you;
For I _ _ drafted to protect
_ Nation, and the Weaker Sect."

_ _ _ _ _ _ _ _ _
_ _ _ _ _ _ _ _
_ _ _ _ _ _ _
_ _ _ _ _ _
_ _ _ _ _
_ _, _ _
_ _' _
_ _
_

Want help?

Turn to page 187 for clues to the longest missing word.

O Say Can You See?... Well, Not Often

The Eagle screameth, while my son
In cashmere uniform has fun.
He marches to the dame he's hot on,
And charms her with the duds he's got on—
Yet harms her not, nor mars her virtue;
He says, "Ma's right; I mustn't hurt you;
For I am drafted to protect
A Nation, and the Weaker Sect."

S C R E A M E T H
C A S H M E R E
M A R C H E S
C H A R M S
H A R M S
M A R S
M A'S
A M
A

Thank Heaven It Was Only a Nightmare

I dreamed that I _ ditch was _ _,
And swam about on fishy _ _ _;
I could not _ _ _ _ my heels or toes—
What _ _ _ _ _ had made away with those?
A fish, dear _ _ _ _ _ _ I seemed to be!—
A nice, _ _ _ _ _ _ _ old man like me
Had, I _ _ _ _ _ _ _ _ _, got in that ditch
For not _ _ _ _ _ _ _ _ _ to some witch.

_

_ _

_ _ _

_ _ _ _

_ _ _ _ _

_ _ _ _ _ _

_ _ _ _ _ _ _

_ _ _ _ _ _ _ _

_ _ _ _ _ _ _ _ _

Want help?
Turn to page 187 for clues to the longest missing word.

Thank Heaven It Was Only a Nightmare

I dreamed that I a ditch was in,
And swam about on fishy fin;
I could not find my heels or toes—
What fiend had made away with those?
A fish, dear friend, I seemed to be!—
A nice, refined old man like me
Had, I inferred, got in that ditch
For not deferring to some witch.

I
IN
FIN
FIND
FIEND
FRIEND
REFINED
INFERRED
DEFERRING

Sans Peur et Sans Reproche

A knight _ _ _ _ _ _ _ _ _ through a glade;
He felt _ _ _ _ _ _ _ _ and much ashamed
That ladies sought him in the shade.
"Has ever knight been so _ _ _ _ _ _ _?
I'm _ _ _ _ _ _ if I, named Galahad,
Shall be _ _ _ _ coxcomb now," he claimed.
I tell you, Galahad was _ _ _!
Yet did the thing upon the spot
His _ _ had said _ knight must not.

_ _ _ _ _ _ _ _ _
_ _ _ _ _ _ _ _
_ _ _ _ _ _ _
_ _ _ _ _ _
_ _ _ _ _
_ _ _ _
_ _ _
_ _
_

Want help?
Turn to page 187 for clues to the longest missing word.

Sans Peur et Sans Reproche

A knight meandered through a glade;
He felt demeaned and much ashamed
That ladies sought him in the shade.
"Has ever knight been so endamed?
I'm damned if I, named Galahad,
Shall be made coxcomb now," he claimed.
I tell you, Galahad was mad!
Yet did the thing upon the spot
His ma had said a knight must not.

M E A N D E R E D
D E M E A N E D
E N D A M E D
D A M N E D
N A M E D —DEAMS
M A D E DAME
M A D
M A
A

The Pierian Spring Is More Intoxicating

— hard it is _ _ reach the _ _ _,
The _ _ _ _ all _ _ _ _ _ quarry at;
E'en those who're _ _ _ _ _ _, asked to stop,
_ _ _ _ _ _ _ they need not touch a drop,
But feel it _ _ _ _ _ _ _ _ to hop
From drunkard clear to laureate—
A stand they won't give up before
They're kicked on the _ _ _ _ _ _ _ _ _.

—
— —
— — —
— — — —
— — — — —
— — — — — —
— — — — — — —
— — — — — — — —
— — — — — — — — —

Want help?
Turn to page 187 for clues to the longest missing word.

The Pierian Spring Is More Intoxicating

O hard it is to reach the top,
The spot all poets quarry at;
E'en those who're topers, asked to stop,
Riposte they need not touch a drop,
But feel it sportier to hop
From drunkard clear to laureate—
A stand they won't give up before
They're kicked on the posterior.

TO
TOP
SPOT
POETS
TOPERS
RIPOSTE
SPORTIER
POSTERIOR

She May Not Think I'm Perfect, Either

Her _ _ _ _ _ _ _ _ _ even me amaze:
She walks her dog while she _ _ _ _ _ _ _ _,
Lights _ _ _ _ _ _ _ when the morning comes,
And in the _ _ _ _ _ _ of love beats drums.
In _ _ _ _ _, she's such an addled lot,
Some folks would like to see her _ _ _ _.
She's not too _ _ _, _ _ say the least;
But _! I love the silly beast.

_ _ _ _ _ _ _ _ _
_ _ _ _ _ _ _ _
_ _ _ _ _ _ _
_ _ _ _ _ _
_ _ _ _ _
_ _ _ _
_ _ _
_ _
_

Want help?
Turn to page 187 for clues to the longest missing word.

She May Not Think I'm Perfect, Either

Her crotchets even me amaze:
She walks her dog while she crochets,
Lights torches when the morning comes,
And in the throes of love beats drums.
In short, she's such an addled lot,
Some folks would like to see her shot.
She's not too hot, to say the least;
But O! I love the silly beast.

CROTCHETS
CROCHETS
TORCHES
THROES
SHORT
SHOT
HOT
TO
O

Not True: She Was Delighted

— hear that Annie, cognizant
She preggers was (_._., enceinte),
Spoke out in _ _ _ on her condition:
"Of things that rile me, parturition
Beats all!" she cried; "it swells my _ _ _ _ _!"
(And more such _ _ _ _ _ _, God forgive her.)
So she _ _ _ _ _ _ _ her fate, and shivered,
And felt _ _ _ _ _ _ _ _ _ to be _ _ _ _ _ _ _ _ _.

I
I.E.
IRE
RILE
LIVER
DRIVEL
REVILED
RELIEVED
DELIVERED

Want help?
Turn to page 187 for clues to the longest missing word.

Not True: She Was Delighted

I hear that Annie, cognizant
She preggers was (i.e., enceinte),
Spoke out in ire on her condition:
"Of things that rile me, parturition
Beats all!" she cried; "it swells my liver!"
(And more such drivel, God forgive her.)
So she reviled her fate, and shivered,
And felt relieved to be delivered.

I
I.E.
IRE
RILE
LIVER
DRIVEL
REVILED
RELIEVED
DELIVERED

A Taste of His Own Medicine, Maybe?

A student of _ _ _ _ _ _ _ _ _ lore
_ _ _ _ _ _ _ _ doctors hated.
He said, "You've my _ _ _ _ _ _ _ for
Your course; I'm _ _ _ _ _ _ for learning, nor
Dare _ _ _ _ _ like you show me the door!—
You're vastly overrated."
'Twas but a _ _ _ _, alas, a _ _ _
To ego; _ _ he got the chop—
_, how humiliated!

_ _ _ _ _ _ _ _ _
_ _ _ _ _ _ _ _
_ _ _ _ _ _ _
_ _ _ _ _ _
_ _ _ _ _
_ _ _ _
_ _ _
_ _
_

Want help?
Turn to page 187 for clues to the longest missing word.

A Taste of His Own Medicine, Maybe?

A student of postmedic lore
Despotic doctors hated.
He said, "You've my deposit for
Your course; I'm poised for learning, nor
Dare dopes like you show me the door!—
You're vastly overrated."
'Twas but a pose, alas, a sop
To ego; so he got the chop—
O, how humiliated!

POSTMEDIC
DESPOTIC
DEPOSIT
POISED
DOPES
POSE
SOP
SO
O

Clever of Mother Nature, Don't You Think?

_ find _ _ odd, as others must,
That when the wedding _ _ _ is knotted,
So many think the _ _ _ _ is just
A good excuse for getting potted.

Vows do not newlyweds _ _ _ _ _,
Or turn to _ _ _ _ _ _ her or him;
It strikes the careful _ _ _ _ _ _ _
That bride and groom seem far from grim.

But their _ _ _ _ _ _ _ _ makes it plain
_ _ _ _ _ _ _ _'_ starting up again.

_
_ _
_ _ _
_ _ _ _
_ _ _ _ _
_ _ _ _ _ _
_ _ _ _ _ _ _
_ _ _ _ _ _ _ _
_ _ _ _ _ _ _ _'_

Want help?
Turn to page 187 for clues to the longest missing word.

Clever of Mother Nature, Don't You Think?

I find it odd, as others must,
That when the wedding tie is knotted,
So many think the rite is just
A good excuse for getting potted.

Vows do not newlyweds inter,
Or turn to cretin her or him;
It strikes the careful noticer
That bride and groom seem far from grim.

But their reaction makes it plain
Creation's starting up again.

I
I T
T I E
R I T E
I N T E R
C R E T I N
N O T I C E R
R E A C T I O N
C R E A T I O N'S

I Hope He Did Not Get Into Heaven

When Doctor X _ _ _ _ _ _ _ _ _ with glee
　　The deadly ailments he'd _ _ _ _ _ _ _ _
　　By cathetering my inside,
　　He much my wicked id _ _ _ _ _ _ _,
And swore it soon must finish me.
　　　　He even went on to _ _ _ _ _ _
　　My face as wrinkled, wizened, _ _ _ _ _.
　　But the _ _ _ _ woe he prophesied
　　Befell not me but him — he died;
I'm _ _ _ of him. On his debris
My _ _ and _ dance merrily.

_ _ _ _ _ _ _ _ _
_ _ _ _ _ _ _ _
_ _ _ _ _ _ _
_ _ _ _ _ _
_ _ _ _ _
_ _ _ _
_ _ _
_ _
_

Want help?

Turn to page 187 for clues to the longest missing word.

I Hope He Did Not Get Into Heaven

When Doctor X described with glee
    The deadly ailments he'd descried
    By cathetering my inside,
    He much my wicked id decried,
And swore it soon must finish me.
    He even went on to deride
    My face as wrinkled, wizened, dried.
    But the dire woe he prophesied
    Befell not me but him—he died;
I'm rid of him. On his debris
My id and I dance merrily.

D E S C R I B E D
D E S C R I E D
D E C R I E D
D E R I D E
D R I E D
D I R E
R I D
I D
I

Odysseus and Circe Revisited

Odysseus, _ _ _ _ _ _ _ _ by Circe, sought
With this _ _ _ _ _ _ _ _ to win the sorceress:
"I've _ _ _ _ _ _ to war and sailed the seas; but nought
Has _ _ _ _ _'_ me so till now; come, let's undress!"

She, fearing to be _ _ _ _'_ if at his mercy,
Said, "First, let's drink," and offered him a _ _ _ _.
He tossed it off, and turned into a _ _ _
(Or, I _ _ told, he seemed _ ram to Circe).

_ _ _ _ _ _ _ _ _
_ _ _ _ _ _ _ _
_ _ _ _ _, _ _
_ _ _ _ _,' _
_ _ _ _' _
_ _ _ _
_ _ _
_ _
_

Want help?
Turn to page 187 for clues to the longest missing word.

Odysseus and Circe Revisited

Odysseus, becharmed by Circe, sought
With this demarche to win the sorceress:
"I've marched to war and sailed the seas; but nought
Has charm'd me so till now; come, let's undress!"

She, fearing to be harm'd if at his mercy,
Said, "First, let's drink," and offered him a dram.
He tossed it off, and turned into a ram
(Or, I am told, he seemed a ram to Circe).

B E C H A R M E D
D E M A R C H E
M A R C H E D
C H A R M'D
H A R M'D
D R A M
R A M
A M
A

She Broadcasts in a Parka When It Is Snowing

Be not _ _ _ _ _ _ _ _ _ _ in crying blues
At this, the _ _ _ _ _ _ _ _ _ of news:
Jane's been _ _ _ _ _ _ _ _! (she who
   _ _ _ _ _ _ _

By holding up a weather card!—
Whose blue eyes _ _ _ _ _ _ _ and shot sweet
   _ _ _ _

   With _ _ _ _ that won all viewers' hearts!)
Some _ _ _   _ _ showtime said _ pro performer
Would shed her clothes when saying, "Fair and warmer."

_ _ _ _ _ _ _ _ _ _
_ _ _ _ _ _ _ _ _ _
_ _ _ _ _ _ _ _ _
_ _ _ _ _ _ _
_ _ _ _ _ _
_ _ _ _ _
_ _ _ _
_ _ _
_ _
_

Want help?
Turn to page 187 for clues to the longest missing word.

She Broadcasts in a Parka When It Is Snowing

Be not restrained in crying blues
At this, the dreariest of news:
Jane's been arrested! (she who starred
By holding up a weather card!—
Whose blue eyes stared, and shot sweet darts
With arts that won all viewers' hearts!)
Some rat at showtime said a pro performer
Would shed her clothes when saying, "Fair and warmer."

RESTRAINED
DREARIEST
ARRESTED
STARRED
STARED
DARTS
ARTS
RAT
AT
A

Joan of Arc Was Much the Same Sort

_ question I _ _ asked: what President
Abandons the Folies-Bergère for Lent,
Lest naughty sights should _ _ _ his concentration
On _ _ _ _*, and other perils to the nation?
He claims the _ _ _ _ _ of papers on his desk
Preclude all idle _ _ _ _ _ _ about burlesque.
_ _ _ _ _ _ _ him not!—the Devil he outwits:
Desire thrown out he never _ _ _ _ _ _ _ _.
Libido skulks away when he commands:
_ _ _ _ _ _ _ _ _ ** not to minds like
_ _ _ _ _ _ _ _ _ _'_.

*War, metaphorically.
** The missing letters are divided into two words here.

—
— —
— — —
— — — —
— — — — —
— — — — — —
— — — — — — —
— — — — — — — —
— — /_ _ _ _ _ _ _
— — — — — — — — — _'_

Want help?
Turn to page 187 for clues to the longest missing word.

Joan of Arc Was Much the Same Sort

A question I am asked: what President
Abandons the Folies-Bergère for Lent,
Lest naughty sights should mar his concentration
On Mars, and other perils to the nation?
He claims the reams of papers on his desk
Preclude all idle dreams about burlesque.
Misread him not!—the Devil he outwits:
Desire thrown out he never readmits.
Libido skulks away when he commands:
Id matters not to minds like Mitterand's.

A
AM
MAR
MARS
REAMS
DREAMS
MISREAD
READMITS
ID/MATTERS
MITTERAND'S

The Cricket and the Ant: A Sequel

_ Cricket to _ _   _ _ _ paid this address:
"Do not, Sir, _ _ _ _ at me for shiftlessness—
You'll set in _ _ _ _ _ events that you may rue;
My _ _ _ _ _ _, Sir, is One, and yours but Two."
Replied the Ant, "You _ _ _ _ _ _ _! —not by chance
(Since charity is _ _ _ _ _ _ _ _ to Ants)
When you were _ _ _ _ _ _ _ _ _ this winter past,
About to perish in the icy blast,
Did I preserve you till the warmth of spring.
Stop railing, Cricket, and start _ _ _ _ _ _ _ _ _ _ _."

_
_ _
_ _ _
_ _ _ _
_ _ _ _ _
_ _ _ _ _ _
_ _ _ _ _ _ _
_ _ _ _ _ _ _ _
_ _ _ _ _ _ _ _ _
_ _ _ _ _ _ _ _ _ _

Want help?
Turn to page 187 for clues to the longest missing word.

The Cricket and the Ant: A Sequel

A Cricket to an Ant paid this address:
"Do not, Sir, rant at me for shiftlessness—
You'll set in train events that you may rue;
My rating, Sir, is One, and yours but Two."
Replied the Ant, "You ingrate!—not by chance
(Since charity is integral to Ants)
When you were faltering this winter past,
About to perish in the icy blast,
Did I preserve you till the warmth of spring.
Stop railing, Cricket, and start flattering."

A
AN
ANT
RANT
TRAIN
RATING
INGRATE
INTEGRAL
FALTERING
FLATTERING

But He Really Did Feel Sympathetic

Sobbed _ cat, _ _ work eating a _ _ _,
"Your _ _ _ _ could not save you your breath;
Your _ _ _ _ _ and your dashes fell flat;
You _ _ _ _ _ _ in my eyes, and saw Death.
You'd strutted and _ _ _ _ _ _ _ _ a few years,
But your life was _ _ _ _ _ _ _ _ by fate."
Though the cat shed the _ _ _ _ _ _ _ _ _ _ tears,
He wasn't _ _ _ _ _ _ _ _ _ _ _ as he ate.

—

— —

— — —

— — — —

— — — — —

— — — — — —

— — — — — — —

— — — — — — — —

— — — — — — — — —

— — — — — — — — — —

Want help?
Turn to page 187 for clues to the longest missing word.

But He Really Did Feel Sympathetic

Sobbed a cat, at work eating a rat,
"Your arts could not save you your breath;
Your darts and your dashes fell flat;
You stared in my eyes, and saw Death.
You'd strutted and starred a few years,
But your life was arrested by fate."
Though the cat shed the dreariest tears,
He wasn't restrained as he ate.

A
AT
RAT
ARTS
DARTS
STARED
STARRED
ARRESTED
DREARIEST
RESTRAINED

At Least He Knows What He likes

_ critic _ _ an _ _ _ display
Could scarcely _ _ _ _ himself away;
He said, "I'll _ _ _ _ _ my Paul Gaugin
With _ _ _ _ _ _ joy for your Dérain.
To excellence my eye is _ _ _ _ _ _ _ _;
I know the honest from the _ _ _ _ _ _ _ _;
Your canvas is _ _ _ _ _ _ _ _ _ _, I see,
But that does not _ _ _ _ _ _ _ _ _ _ me."

_
_ _
_ _ _
_ _ _ _
_ _ _ _ _
_ _ _ _ _ _
_ _ _ _ _ _ _
_ _ _ _ _ _ _ _
_ _ _ _ _ _ _ _ _
_ _ _ _ _ _ _ _ _ _

Want help?
Turn to page 187 for clues to the longest missing word.

At Least He Knows What He likes

A critic at an art display
Could scarcely tear himself away;
He said, "I'll trade my Paul Gaugin
With ardent joy for your Dérain.
To excellence my eye is trained;
I know the honest from the strained;
Your canvas is restained, I see,
But that does not dishearten me."

A
AT
ART
TEAR
TRADE
ARDENT
TRAINED
STRAINED
RESTRAINT
DISHEARTEN

Note Found Under a Pillar in Italy

Sir:

    _, black slave, who perished _ _
A Roman game, amid the _ _ _
Of crowds that when the bell went "_ _ _ _!"
Roared, "Die, _ _ _ _ _, die!"—I, vanished thing
Whom none recalls—to you whose _ _ _ _ _ _
Is coming soon enough, am _ _ _ _ _ _ _
This word: Though you'll see _ _ _ _ _ _ _ _ grim,
See _ _ _ _ _ _ _ _ _ _ of limb from limb,
Remain, as I did, _ _ _ _ _ _ _ _ _ _ _,
Until you join the

        _ _ _ _ _ _ _ _ _ _ _.

(I have no evidence that the Roman emperors rang a bell to start the games. But why not?)

  _
  _ _
  _ _ _
  _ _ _ _
  _ _ _ _ _
  _ _ _ _ _ _
  _ _ _ _ _ _ _
  _ _ _ _ _ _ _ _
  _ _ _ _ _ _ _ _ _
  _ _ _ _ _ _ _ _ _ _

Want help?
Turn to page 187 for clues to the longest missing word.

Note Found Under a Pillar in Italy

Sir:
    I, black slave, who perished in
A Roman game, amid the din
Of crowds that when the bell went "Ding!"
Roared, "Die, dinge, die!" — I, vanished thing
Whom none recalls — to you whose ending
Is coming soon enough, am sending
This word: Though you'll see rendings grim,
See sundering of limb from limb,
Remain, as I did, unresigned,
Until you join the
                    Undersigned.

I
IN
DIN
DING
DINGE
ENDING
SENDING
RENDINGS
SUNDERING
UNRESIGNED
UNDERSIGNED

Sonnet to My Mistress Before Hanging

Not even _ _ _ _ _ _ _ _ _ _ _ _ _ _ _ 'tis
That I life's dear _ _ _ _ _ _ _ _ _ _ _ _ _ _ must
Forsake, while you, my _ _ _ _ _ _ _-_ _ _ _ _ Ms.,
Still play at puns and _ _ _ _ _ _ _ _ _ _ _ and lust
Just as we two have played. _ _ _ _ _ _ _ _ _ _
Our fumblings were; their _ _ _ _ _ _ _ _ _ chill
Helped noose this _ _ _ _ _ _ _ _, dangling here to haul
Me hellward. Yet the _ _ _ _ _ _ _ was not you;
All lovers buy such _ _ _ _ _ _. It befell
That God _ _ _ _ _ me, not you, away from life,
And bids me not to _ _ _ _, but sink to hell.
(Wait! Who's that whispers, "_ _ _, I'd be your wife,
For it _ _ lonely when the shadows fall"?
Perhaps _ will not hang me after all.)

_ _ _ _ _ _ _ _ _ _ _ _ _ _ _
_ _ _ _ _ _ _ _ _ _ _ _ _ _
_ _ _ _ _ _ _-_ _ _ _ _
_ _ _ _ _ _ _ _ _ _ _ _
_ _ _ _ _ _ _ _ _ _ _
_ _ _ _ _ _ _ _ _
_ _ _ _ _ _ _ _
_ _ _ _ _ _ _
_ _ _ _ _ _
_ _ _ _ _
_ _ _ _
_ _ _
_ _
_

Want help?
Turn to page 187 for clues to the longest missing word.

Sonnet to My Mistress Before Hanging

Not even semipardonable 'tis
That I life's dear imponderables must
Forsake, while you, my promise-laden Ms.,
Still play at puns and palindromes and lust
Just as we two have played. Impersonal
Our fumblings were; their semipolar chill
Helped noose this sailrope, dangling here to haul
Me hellward. Yet the spoiler was not you;
All lovers buy such perils. It befell
That God pries me, not you, away from life,
And bids me not to rise, but sink to hell.
(Wait! Who's that whispers, "Sir, I'd be your wife,
For it is lonely when the shadows fall"?
Perhaps I will not hang me after all.)

SEMIPARDONABLE
IMPONDERABLES
PROMISE-LADEN
PALINDROMES
IMPERSONAL
SEMIPOLAR
SAILROPE
SPOILER
PERILS
PRIES
RISE
SIR
IS
I

A Word from a Man of Mighty Mind

_ reader, know! _ _ fool I be,
But monstrous in mentality.
As _ _ _ after eon speeds,
My _ _ _ _ for logic none exceeds.
As _ _ _ _ _ is honeyed o'er with jam,
So I with sine and _ _ _ _ _ _ am.
To medics I no _ _ _ _ _ _ pay—
I know _ _ _ _ _ _ _ _ well as they.
I know _ _ _ _ _ _ _ _ _ _ damage genes,
_ _ _ _ _ _ _ _ _ _ _ blow to smithereens,
And _ _ _ _ _ _ _ _ _ _ _ _ skip the ear.
To me such _ _ _ _ _ _ _ _ _ _ _ _ _ is dear.
The _ _ _ _ _ _ _ _ _ _ _ _ _ _ _ cause, I guess,
My mental state's _ _ _ _ _ _ _ _ _ _ _ _ _ _ _ _ .

_

_ _

_ _ _

_ _ _ _

_ _ _ _ _

_ _ _ _ _ _

_ _ _ _ _ _ _

_ _ _ _ _ _ _ _

_ _ _ _ _ _ _ _ _

_ _ _ _ _ _ _ _ _ _

_ _ _ _ _ _ _ _ _ _ _

_ _ _ _ _ _ _ _ _ _ _ _

_ _ _ _ _ _ _ _ _ _ _ _ _

Want help?

Turn to page 187 for clues to the longest missing word.

A Word from a Man of Mighty Mind

O reader, know! No fool I be,
But monstrous in mentality.
As eon after eon speeds,
My nose for logic none exceeds.
As scone is honeyed o'er with jam,
So I with sine and cosine am.
To medics I no cession pay—
I know necrosis well as they.
I know incrosses damage genes,
Recussions blow to smithereens,
And supersonics skip the ear.
To me such preciousness is dear.
The repercussions cause, I guess,
My mental state's precariousness.

O
N O
E O N
N O S E
S C O N E
C O S I N E
C E S S I O N
N E C R O S I S
I N C R O S S E S
R E C U S S I O N S
S U P E R S O N I C S
P R E C I O U S N E S S
R E P E R C U S S I O N S
P R E C A R I O U S N E S S

What Does "The" Mean, for Instance?

From low-grade childhood _ _ _ _ _ _ _ _ _ _ _ _ _ _
Much _ _ _ _ _ _ _ _ _ _ _ _ _ for me dates—
I never learned the denotations
Of big words like "_ _ _ _ _ _ _ _ _ _ _ ."
"_ _ _ _ _ _ _ _ _ _ _ _," now, I know, and take
"_ _ _ _ _ _ _ _ _ _ _" quite in my stride,
While "_ _ _ _ _ _ _ _ _," that's a piece of cake.
There are some shorter words I've tried—
"_ _ _ _ _ _ _ _," which means just "broads a train;"
And "_ _ _ _ _ _ _," too harsh to say;
"_ _ _ _ _ _" means "to the rear"—that's plain.
Yet flow, _ _ _ _ _ flow! It _ _ _ _ my heart away
That I'm still stumped by "_ _ _," and "_ _," and "_."

_ _ _ _ _ _ _ _ _ _ _ _ _ _
_ _ _ _ _ _ _ _ _ _ _ _ _
_ _ _ _ _ _ _ _ _ _ _ _
_ _ _ _ _ _ _ _ _ _ _
_ _ _ _ _ _ _ _ _ _
_ _ _ _ _ _ _ _ _
_ _ _ _ _ _ _ _
_ _ _ _ _ _ _
_ _ _ _ _ _
_ _ _ _ _
_ _ _ _
_ _ _
_ _
_

Want help?
Turn to page 187 for clues to the longest missing word.

What Does "The" Mean, for Instance?

From low-grade childhood concentrations
Much consternation for me dates—
I never learned the denotations
Of big words like "contorniates."
"Transection," now, I know, and take
"Stentorian" quite in my stride,
While "transient," that's a piece of cake.
There are some shorter words I've tried—
"Entrains," which means just "boards a train;"
And "nastier," too harsh to say;
"Astern" means "to the rear"—that's plain.
Yet flow, tears, flow! It eats my heart away
That I'm still stumped by "sea," and "as," and "a."

CONCENTRATIONS
CONSTERNATION
CONTORNIATES
TRANSECTION
STENTORIAN
TRANSIENT
ENTRAINS
NASTIER
ASTERN
TEARS
EATS
SEA
AS
A

Clues to the ESPYramids

Doris Nash Wortman prefaced her acrostic puzzles in the New York Times with the remark that she used reference books in making her puzzles, and that her readers were welcome to use reference books in solving them. I present these ESPYramid clues in the same spirit. The chances are against your bogging down in any of the verses, but in case you do I would much rather have you take one small hint and start again than give up and throw my book in the trash can. (There is an even quicker way to arrive at a solution. You can turn to the completed verse—it's on the page following each puzzle—for the complete answers, fill in all the blanks, and then tell your friends how quick you were. But I doubt whether you would find that very gratifying.)

Each ESPYramid is listed below, according to its page number. The letters of the longest missing word in each verse are arranged in alphabetical order, so that you can figure out the word just by juggling the letters. And the "definitions" should help, though I've tried to make them something of a challenge too.

97. It's All My Own Fault. G H H O T T U. Einstein was good at it.
99. And Think of All the Chances He Has! A A I N R S T. He sings well, too.
101. When He Went Off His Diet, He Overdid It. A D D E E S T. It was the only way to keep him quiet.
103. Good Night, Good Knight. D N N O S U W. One of those diurnal happenings.
105. And You're Not Perfect, Either. A D F G I N R T. Drawing up a preliminary version.
107. He Was Finally Expelled. A C E E H R S T. They'll take you in if you don't take them out first.
109. It's Worth Considering These Nuclear Days. A A C E M R S S. What the Yankees did regularly to other baseball teams a long time ago.
111. Faith Rewarded. A A D E I P R S. Better than the other place.

113. I Remember When You Did the Same, Dear. A E I P R S S T. The best prepared.

115. Frankly, I'd Prefer a Rocking Horse. A D E E I R S T. The best prepared.

117. Unlikely Litany. A D E E G N R V. Carved, etched.

119. He Should Have Counted to Ten First. A D E I O R S T. He wound up out of breath, between Mars and Venus.

121. The U.N. Wouldn't Permit It Nowadays. D E F I L N R S. He was an English navigator and explorer (1774–1814).

123. But I Suppose They Do Have Fun Sometimes. A C E E H R S T. They have not changed their ways since "He Was Finally Expelled," page 107.

125. He Wasn't for Sale, Though. A E G G I R S T. Most tattered.

127. Chance Spins the Wheel. A E N P R S T T. Arrangements having or suggesting a design.

129. And They're Smooth Going Down. A A C E E L R T. To mangle.

131. We Both Go to Bed Hungry. A E H R S S T V. Crops, that is.

133. There's Gold in Them Sandlots. A D F G I N R T. Selecting from a group.

135. Schizophrenia, No Doubt. A D D D E E M N. Drove insane.

137. How *Can* You Do Worse? C D D E E I R T. Given credit.

139. Perhaps We Need More Idlers Like That. E F I L R R S T. Their actions have no serious purpose.

141. I Can't Even Get Into the Saddle. D E I R S S S T. A state of anxiety or sorrow.

143. Envy at Eighty. E E I O P R R S T. Curtains for doorways.

145. The Word Does Mean Christian, You Know. A C E I N O R S T. The process of bringing into being, in a possessive sort of way.

147. I Didn't Know Bedouins Wore Them. A E E I L N P S T. I wish they would stop fighting over there.

149. O Say Can You See? . . . Well, Not Often. A C E E H M R S T. Uttereth a piercing cry.

151. Thank Heaven It Was Only a Nightmare. D E E F G I N R R. When he passed her, he should have tipped his hat.

153. Sans Peur et Sans Reproche. A D D E E E M N R. He really was not going anywhere.

155. The Pierian Spring Is More Intoxicating. E I O O P R R S T. To a yachtsman it would be the stern.

157. She May Not Think I'm Perfect, Either. C C E H O R S T T. Eccentricities.

159. Not True: She Was Delighted. D D E E E I L R V. Rescued from bondage, according to some.

161. A Taste of His Own Medicine, Maybe? C D E I M O P S T. He already had his M.D.

163. Clever of Mother Nature, Don't You Think? A C E I N O R S T. See "definition" clue for 145, above.

165. I Hope He Did Not Get Into Heaven. B C D D E E I R S. He told all about it.

167. Odysseus and Circe Revisited. A B C D E E H M R. Intoxicated, but not by alcohol.

169. She Broadcasts in a Parka When It Is Snowing. A D E E I N R R S T. Don't be that way—let yourself go!

171. Joan of Arc Was Much the Same Sort. A D E I M N R S T T. Frenchmen are familiar with the name.

173. The Cricket and the Ant: A Sequel. A E F G I L N R T T. President Nixon called it "stroking."

175. But He Really Did Feel Sympathetic. A D E E I N R R S T. Held in check.

177. At Least He Knows What He Likes. A D E E I H N R S T. To discourage.

179. Note Found Under a Pillar in Italy. D D E E G I N N R S U. That, and under ground too.

181. Sonnet to My Mistress Before Hanging. A A B D E E I L M N O P R S. Partly excusable.

183. A Word from a Man of Mighty Mind. A C E E I N O P R R S S S U. Lack of security or stability.

185. What Does "The" Mean, for Instance? A C C E I N N N O O R S T T. Close attention more than once.

Index of Verse/Puzzles, by Title

· 191 ·